WORLD MYTHS

KENNETH C. DAVIS
ILLUSTRATED BY SERGIO RUZZIER

HarperCollins*Publishers*

Every effort has been made to secure permission to reprint the excerpts contained in this book. The publisher gratefully acknowledges the following:

The quote on page 11 [JUNG] is reprinted from *Memories, Dreams, and Reflections* by C. G. Jung, recorded and edited by Aniela Jaffé, translated from the German by Richard and Clara Winston, published by Pantheon Books.

The quote on page 21 [GILGAMESH] is an excerpt from Kovacs, Maureen Gallery, translator, *The Epic of Gilgamesh*, with an Introduction and Notes copyright © 1985, 1989, by the Board of Trustees of the Leland Stanford Junior University. Used with the permission of Stanford University Press, www.sup.org.

The quotes on pages 46–47 [ILIAD] and 49 [ODYSSEY] are reprinted from Great Books of the Western World, copyright 1952, 1990 Encyclopaedia Britannica, Inc.

The quote on page 63 [MAHABHARATA] is reprinted from *Mahabharata*, retold by William Buck, published by the University of California Press, copyright © 1973 by the Regents of the University of California.

The quote on pages 108–109 [PROSE EDDA] is reprinted from *The Prose Edda of Snorri Sturluson: Tales from Norse Mythology*, selected and translated by Jean I. Young, published by the University of California Press, copyright © 1964 by the Regents of the University of California.

Photo credits: page 81, *Warlukurlangu Jukurrpa* (*Fire Country Dreaming*) by Rosie Nangala Flemming. (WA507228/Aboriginal, Northern Territory, Australia, Oceania, 1995.) Photograph reproduced with the kind permission of the Royal Pavilion, Libraries and Museums (Brighton and Hove), United Kingdom. All other photographs courtesy of the Library of Congress.

Library of Congress Cataloging-in-Publication Data
Davis, Kenneth C.
  Don't know much about world myths / Kenneth C. Davis ; illustrated by Sergio Ruzzier.—1st ed.
      p.   cm. — (Don't know much about)
  Includes index.
  ISBN 0-06-028605-9 — ISBN 0-06-028606-7 (lib. bdg.) — ISBN 0-06-440837-X (pbk.)
  1. Mythology—Juvenile literature.   I. Ruzzier, Sergio.   II. Title.
BL312.D38 2005   2004016137
201'.3—dc22

Design by Charles Yuen
1 2 3 4 5 6 7 8 9 10

First Edition

—ACKNOWLEDGMENTS—

An author's name goes on the cover of a book. But behind the book are a great many people who make it all happen. I would like to thank all the wonderful people at HarperCollins who helped make this book a reality, including Susan Katz, Kate Morgan Jackson, Barbara Lalicki, Harriet Barton, Rosemary Brosnan, Amy Burton, Meredith Charpentier, Dana Hayward, Maggie Herold, Jeanne Hogle, Rachel Orr, Lorelei Russ, and Sarah Thomson. I would also like to thank David Black, Joy Tutela, and Alix Reid for their friendship, assistance, and great ideas. My wife, Joann, and my children, Jenny and Colin, are always a source of inspiration, joy, and support, and without them my work would not be possible.

I especially thank Jennifer Hart, graduate student in religious studies at Indiana University, for reviewing the manuscript; Bhawna Ojha, for providing helpful insights; Sergio Ruzzier for his clever illustrations; and April Prince for her unique contribution. This book would not have been possible without her tireless work, imagination, and creativity.

— CONTENTS —

Statue of Apollo

When I was in fifth grade, I found it impossible to sit still during class. I fidgeted at my desk as the clock ticked slowly and loudly toward three o'clock and freedom. I didn't pay much attention to the teacher, except for the few minutes at the end of each day when she set aside math and science to read from *The Odyssey*.

Apart from recess, this was my only moment of joy during the long school day. As my teacher read, the clock disappeared and the chalkboard vanished. Instead of fighting fractions and verbs in the classroom, I was on board a Greek ship, sailing mythical oceans, combating witches and demons—trying to find my way home with brave Odysseus, the wily hero of Homer's epic.

Those daily doses gave me a hunger for more mythology. I spent hours in the library, devouring stories of the Norse trickster Loki and the Egyptian gods who inspired the pyramids. I had discovered a whole new world, and it interested me a lot more than school did!

Don't Know Much About® World Myths includes a wealth of these remarkable, ancient stories of gods and goddesses, spirits and supernatural monsters, great heroes and heroines. These myths include battles, quests, and romances; like the tales we enjoy today, they are filled with excitement, danger, courage, loyalty, friendship, and love.

Besides reading myths for entertainment, we can read myths to learn more about the past. Almost every culture has a collection of stories about its origin, history, ancestors, gods, and heroes. Some myths served as an early form of history. Others explained nature before science gave us reasons behind the sun and stars, the changing seasons, growing crops, and why people died. And others became the basis for what people believed— their religions. It is important to remember that people have believed different things throughout history.

The world of myths is just as real and alive for me today as it was when I was in fifth grade. That's because these stories from all over the world are full of excitement and adventure. So as you read these fabulous stories from another time, imagine sitting around a campfire three thousand years ago and hearing tales of gods fighting in the heavens and heroes battling monsters. Welcome to the wonderful world of mythology!

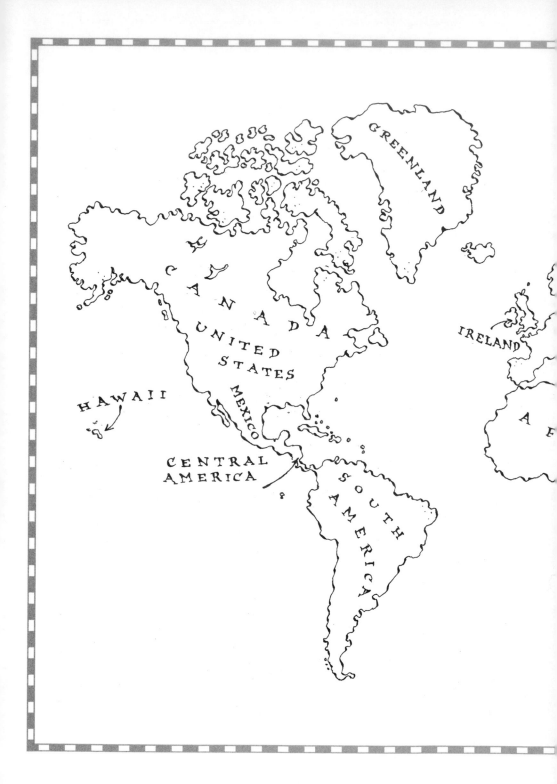

INAVIA
ALY
GREECE
CHINA
JAPAN
INDIA
EGYPT
ICA
MESOPOTAMIA
POLYNESIA
AUSTRALIA
NEW ZEALAND

CHAPTER 1

WHAT IS MYTHOLOGY?

Siegfried faces a dragon in this film based on Norse and Germanic myth.

Are myths true?

It depends on whom you ask—and what you mean by true.

In modern culture, "myth" has come to mean a story or an idea that is *not* true. Today, people speak of myths about how to catch or cure the common cold. But the age-old myths in this book were a vital part of people's religions, cultures, and everyday lives. Often they are both deeply spiritual and entertaining.

To many ancients, their mythology was their history; there was little, if any, distinction between the two. Some myths were actually grounded in historical events—such as floods or wars. Others explain the mysteries of the earth. For example, today we know the scientific reasons for the seasons. But the Greeks' explanation for the change of seasons was that the daughter of the harvest goddess lived in the underworld for part of the year. The goddess was so upset during this time that the earth became barren and cold.

Even though science and technology have explained a lot about how the universe works, we will probably never know much more about human nature or the afterlife than we already do. Myths continue to give us the feeling that we can and do understand the mysteries around us.

Why do we continue to tell ancient myths?

Mythology offers a treasure trove of dramatic tales. And humans, by nature, love stories. We look for them everywhere—in books, movies, plays, television shows, computer games, and mail from friends—because they help us understand other people and the world. Mythology's themes and characters are so universal that we can all relate to them, no matter when, where, or how we live. Myths express our hopes and fears, our strengths and weaknesses. They connect us to people of other times and places by showing us that we are not so different from one another.

MYTHIC VOICES:

❝No science will ever replace myth, and a myth cannot be made out of any science.❞

—SWISS PSYCHOANALYST CARL JUNG

Some myths can be read as *allegories*, or stories filled with symbolic representations. Once you know what to look for, symbols in both allegories and other myths can reveal a lot about a story's meaning. For example, a snake almost always represents rebirth or immortality. Bridges can represent some sort of divide to be crossed. Women are often associated with the earth, and men with the sky.

Is every culture's mythology alike?

Each culture's mythology is unique, but most do share common subjects. Some of these include the creation of the earth; the arrival of the first humans; how humans came to use fire; the journey to, and nature of, the afterlife; heroes and heroines who must battle evil; a massive flood that nearly destroys humankind; and humans' relationship to the gods.

Some cultures' mythologies share more than common subjects—they have specific myths that are similar. This is true of cultures that existed near one another, but also of some half a world apart. How is this so? In many cases, it's clear how different cultures influenced each other. Usually, they were trading partners or had trading partners in common, or one was invading the other. Sometimes, though, the influence is much harder to trace. Some scholars who study myths think that the patterns, themes, and ideas that form the basis of myth may be built in to our brains, making them universal to all people, no matter what their background or culture.

MYTHIC VOICES:

66 There are only two or three human stories, and they go on repeating themselves as fiercely as if they had never happened before. 99

—WILLA CATHER, *O PIONEERS!*

What's the difference between a myth and a folktale? A legend? A fable?

Sometimes it's difficult to tell! All these story forms have things in common. Most often they've been passed on orally, and none of them have authors. But they are not exactly the same.

Myths deal with big questions and issues, such as life and death or the beginning of the universe—things that concern all humans, no matter when or where they live. Unlike the other story forms, myths are generally considered true by the people who create them.

Folktales contain many mythic elements, but they tend to deal with conflicts between people or societies, rather than with cosmic issues. Like myths, folktales entertain people, but they are more likely than myths to reveal a moral about society.

Legends, unlike most myths, describe a supposedly historical figure or event that is said to have happened at a specific time and place in the past. A legend contains elements or themes from a culture's mythology, but it is not incorporated into a culture's belief system the way a myth is.

A fable is perhaps the easiest of these story forms to identify because it has a clear-cut moral attached to it. Myths and folktales sometimes have morals, but they are not usually stated directly.

Who wrote the first myths?

For tens of thousands of years, myths were passed on by word of mouth, handed down from generation to generation by poets or professional storytellers. Some villages appointed a specific storyteller whose job was to learn the group's myths and retell them to educate and entertain the other villagers. There were also traveling storytellers who visited different villages, exchanging stories for food and lodging. As often happens when a story is passed on orally, details change with each teller and each telling. The result is that in many cultures, there are several different versions of the same myth.

The first written myths were those of the Sumerians, who began recording stories of their gods and goddesses in about 2500 B.C.E. Even after writing developed independently in other places around the world, however, only a few members of a society could read and write. Word of mouth remained the best way to communicate with large numbers of people.

Myths have also been passed on through dances, rituals, or drama. They have been expressed in paintings, sculpture, pottery, and other forms of artwork. These different formats for telling and recording myths have left us many ways to learn about and continue telling ancient myths today.

MYTHIC VOICES:

66 Throughout the inhabited world, in all times and under every circumstance, the myths of man have flourished. 99

—JOSEPH CAMPBELL, *THE HERO WITH A THOUSAND FACES*

Are there modern myths?

Humans still want to explain the world and glorify their heroes and achievements, just as the ancients did. One way we do this is through civic myths—stories about a nation's history and heroes that people believe because they want to, even if they know the tales aren't exactly true. Many civic myths of the

United States started out with a grain of truth and were exaggerated over time; others were completely made up. It is a myth, for example, that the young George Washington chopped down his father's cherry tree and then said, "I cannot tell I lie; I did it with my hatchet." This story was invented by one of Washington's biographers to show how honest George was. Other American myths include Betsy Ross sewing the first American flag (she did sew flags, though almost certainly not the first one) and the Pilgrims first stepping ashore in the New World at an impressive boulder called Plymouth Rock. (The Pilgrims landed on Cape Cod before moving on to Plymouth and, though it's possible that they stepped on the rock, it's more likely that they just landed somewhere near it.) Despite their inaccuracies, these civic myths help bind the United States together as a nation by creating a common history.

Traditional mythic characters, heroes, and elements also appear in novels and other stories. Filmmaker George Lucas has said, "With *Star Wars* I consciously set about to re-create myths and the classic mythological motifs. I wanted to use those motifs to deal with issues that exist today. . . . The issues are the same ones that existed three thousand years ago."

Luke Skywalker, Frodo Baggins, Harry Potter, Huckleberry Finn, and Dorothy from Kansas are just a few of the fictional heroes who embark on a quest to achieve a certain goal. Along the way, he or she battles evil in larger-than-life forms and returns a stronger, better person. You can bet that the creators of these characters knew their ancient mythology.

CHAPTER 2

THE MIDDLE EAST

MESOPOTAMIA AND EGYPT

Egyptian pyramids and village during a flood

MESOPOTAMIA

Who lived in Mesopotamia?

The Sumerians were the first to settle in the fertile valley of
Mesopotamia (the area between the Tigris and Euphrates rivers
in modern-day Iraq) in about 5000 B.C.E. Their many city-states
became the world's first civilization, and possibly its first great
empire. Sumerian people made pottery and textiles, became
priests and merchants, built temples and other structures, and
nurtured scholars who thought of new ideas. Some of the things
developed in Mesopotamia include money, a system of weights
and measures, the first world map, the wheel, the first written
calendar, beer, and the world's first known form of writing, a
simple system of wedge-shaped characters called cuneiform.

By about 2000 B.C.E., the Babylonian people had come to
dominate Mesopotamia. They became the area's next great
civilization. The Babylonians remained in Mesopotamia for two
thousand years, absorbing the land of the Sumerians and many
Sumerian beliefs, laws, and ways of life.

Our seven-day week comes from the Babylonians, who believed that seven was a lucky number. The Babylonians were probably the first civilization to study the heavens. They named the days of the week after their gods of the sun, moon, and planets. Later civilizations borrowed this system and replaced the Babylonian names with those of their own gods. Can you guess which heavenly bodies inspired our own names Saturday, Sunday, and Monday? (To learn how the other days of the week got their names, see page 111.)

How did the Babylonians believe the universe began?

In the beginning, the Babylonians said, there was only water and the two gods who ruled it. The god Apsu ruled over sweet, fresh water, and the goddess Tiamat ruled over salt water. Together Apsu and Tiamat had three children. Soon those children had children and grandchildren. Before long there were so many gods and goddesses that Apsu declared the noise would drive him mad. He wanted to kill them all to get some peace and quiet. Tiamat promptly rejected Apsu's evil solution.

When Ea, the god of wisdom, learned of Apsu's plan, he used magic to put Apsu into a deep sleep and kill him. Ea then took Apsu's place as king of fresh water. He and his wife, the goddess Damkina, soon had a son named Marduk.

How did Marduk become the king of the gods?

Ea was so thrilled with his son that he gave the boy four eyes and four ears, so he could see and hear everything going on around him. (Imagine having an eye in the back of your head!) Marduk could also breathe fire.

Tiamat, angry about her husband's death, was determined to get revenge. She assembled an army of ferocious dragons, serpents, and scorpion men, led by her son Kingu. The other gods were terrified. Marduk alone agreed to take on

Tiamat's army. But he had one condition: If he was victorious, the other gods had to make him supreme leader.

As weapons, Marduk took lightning rods, hurricane winds, a net, and a spear into battle. He snared Tiamat in his net. When she opened her mouth to swallow him, Marduk hurled a violent wind into her throat and shot an arrow down the center of her body, piercing her heart and killing her. Marduk threw every last one of Tiamat's monsters into the underworld.

The triumphant new king of the gods then created the world by splitting Tiamat's body in two. With one half, Marduk created the earth; with the other, he made the heavens. Then he made the sun and the moon, arranged the stars in the sky, and divided the year into months. He created rain from Tiamat's saliva, mountains from her head, and the Tigris and Euphrates rivers from her eyes. Before he was through, Marduk molded the first men and women, using clay mixed with the blood of Kingu, and brought the people to life to serve the gods.

 Noah was the first man to build a boat when a flood came.

False. Humans had not been around long when the air god Enlil tired of their noise and rabble. Enlil convinced his fellow gods to flood the earth and do away with humankind.

The god Ea, who was sympathetic to humans, instructed one man named Utanapishtim to tear down his house, build a boat, and put his family and as many living things as possible onto the vessel. Just as Utanapishtim finished loading the boat, rain began to fall. For six days and nights, the rain poured out of the heavens in a storm so terrifying even the gods were afraid of what they'd done. When the rain stopped on the seventh day, the creatures in Utanapishtim's boat were the only ones that hadn't been swallowed up by the flood and turned to mud.

After floating in the endless sea, Utanapishtim's boat finally washed ashore atop Mount Nisir, the only land left above sea level. At first Enlil was furious that humankind survived. But Ea and the other gods reminded him that without humans, the gods would no longer enjoy people's sacrifices and offerings. Enlil acknowledged this truth and decided to reward Utanapishtim by making him and his wife immortal.

WORLD OF WORDS

Mortal means to be subject to death. Humans are sometimes called mortals—unless they are rewarded by the gods. Then, like most gods, they become *immortal* and live forever.

MYTHIC LINKS

The Mesopotamian myth of Utanapishtim is closely related to the Hebrew story of Noah and the Ark. Is it a coincidence? Probably not. The Hebrew people, descendants of the biblical figures Abraham, Isaac, and Jacob, originally came from Mesopotamia and shared a common history with the Babylonians. It's almost certain that the floods recounted in the two stories are the same. Archaeologists have found evidence of an especially devastating Mesopotamian flood that occurred around 4000 B.C.E. and left about eleven feet of mud and silt on top of the Sumerian city of Uruk. Ancient Mesopotamians, with their limited knowledge of the rest of the globe, may have believed that the flood engulfed the entire earth.

Massive floods are one of the most common themes in world mythology. Some cultures believed a flood was sent to destroy humans and their sins; others thought the flood was merely the whim of the gods. A flood was often seen as a devastating event, but one that cleared the way for new creation.

Who is Gilgamesh?

Gilgamesh is a hero of Mesopotamian mythology whom most scholars believe to be based on a real Sumerian king. The most famous story about him is the *Epic of Gilgamesh*. Recorded in sections between 2100 and 627 B.C.E., *Gilgamesh* is the oldest major work of literature in the world.

Gilgamesh, one-third man and two-thirds god, reigned as king of Uruk. He was so energetic that his people could not keep up with him. Nearly at their wits' end, the people went to the gods for help. The gods' solution was to create a companion for Gilgamesh who would be as strong and active as the king.

They made Enkidu, a wild and hairy man who lived in the forest with the animals. Enkidu and Gilgamesh became aware of each other's extraordinary might, and before long the two engaged in a duel. They wrestled for hours in an equal match until Gilgamesh, exhausted, finally fell to one knee. Instead of remaining enemies, however, the two warriors became best friends out of their mutual respect and admiration. Enkidu came to live in the palace with Gilgamesh, and they spent their days battling monsters together.

Why did Gilgamesh search for eternal youth?

Ishtar, the goddess of love and war, sent the Bull of Heaven to kill Gilgamesh for refusing her hand in marriage. Though Gilgamesh and Enkidu fought the Bull of Heaven together, it was Enkidu who dealt the final blow. The two men had to be punished for destroying a being made by the gods. The gods struck Enkidu with a disease, and within days he was dead. Gilgamesh's punishment was to face life without his best friend.

 To Mesopotamians, the snake's eating of the plant of eternal youth in the *Epic of Gilgamesh* explained why snakes shed their skin and become "young" (at least young looking) again.

Enkidu's death made Gilgamesh not only lonely, but also terrified about facing his own death. The king determined to find eternal youth. He made a difficult journey to visit his ancestor Utanapishtim and asked him the secret to staying forever young. After some hesitation, Utanapishtim told Gilgamesh about a magical plant of eternal youth that grew at the bottom of the sea. Gilgamesh dove into the water and picked the plant. Overjoyed, he left for Uruk to share it with his people. But when he stopped at a pool to wash on his way home, a snake slithered out from the grass and ate the plant.

So it happened that Gilgamesh and his people could not get the best of death.

MYTHIC VOICES:

❝I will disclose to you a thing that is hidden, Gilgamesh. . . .

There is a plant . . . like a boxthorn,

whose thorns will prick your hand like a rose.

If your hands reach that plant *you will become a young man again.*❞

— FROM THE *EPIC OF GILGAMESH*, TRANSLATED BY MAUREEN GALLERY KOVACS

What brought Egypt its most precious gifts?

The Nile River brought life to Egypt. Near the river, Egyptians planted vegetables and fruits, grains for making bread and beer, papyrus plants for making paper, and flax plants for making fine linen cloth. The Nile also provided plenty of fish, and mud for making bricks and pottery.

Beyond the farmland was the desert, which held gold, precious gems, and stone. Along with the many gifts from the Nile, these riches helped make Egypt a great empire for three thousand years. Egyptians built enormous stone structures, including the pyramids, to honor their kings. They made jewelry, perfume, and cosmetics. They developed the first known calendar based on 365 days, and an early form of writing called *hieroglyphs*, or picture-writing. Egyptians also had a highly developed religion and studied medicine, astronomy, and engineering.

 The land along the Nile was once home to many separate tribes, each with their own gods. There were more than two thousand gods altogether (though no one person would have worshipped them all, since beliefs and stories were specific to different locations). Even after Egypt was united under one ruler, the pharaoh (king) Menes, around 3100 B.C.E., regional gods remained important to local populations.

Why did Egyptian gods have animal heads?

Early Egyptians believed that the gods existed in the form of animals. Many gods were linked to animals with whom they shared certain characteristics. For example, the moon god of magic and wisdom, Thoth, was associated with a bird called the ibis, which has a beak shaped like a crescent moon. However, the Egyptians did not worship the animals themselves, but the gods who were associated with the animals. Over time the gods gradually took on human bodies but often retained their animal heads.

How did Egyptian myth explain the creation of the universe?

In the beginning, there was only energy and the dark and watery chaos of Nun, a motionless sea. Out of Nun rose the world's first mound of land, the primeval mound. The mound supplied a place for the first god to create himself. This god was the sun god, called Ra or Ra-Atum. After creating himself, Ra realized he was alone. So he made his children, Shu and Tefnut. Shu was the god of air, produced from Ra's sneeze. Tefnut, the goddess of dew and rain, was created from Ra's spit.

Shu and Tefnut together created Geb, the earth god, and Nut, the sky goddess. At first the two lay so close together that there was no room between them for any living things to exist. So Ra ordered Shu to separate them. Geb remained where he was, with the curves of his body forming the peaks and valleys of the earth. Nut was pushed high into the sky, where the underside of her body formed the blue sky of day and the starry heavens of night.

How did Ra make the sun rise each morning? He:

a) sailed across the sky in his sun barque

b) threw a ball of fire into the air

c) willed it to rise with the powers of his mind

The answer is letter *a*. Every morning, after his bath and breakfast, the sun god climbed into a boat called the sun barque for a journey across the sky. It was said that in the morning, Ra was a young boy. At midday, he was a man. And by evening, he had grown old.

Some versions of this myth say that night fell when Ra was swallowed by Nut. He would spent the night traveling through the sky goddess's body until she gave birth to him again each morning. Other versions of the story say that Ra spent the night traveling through the underworld, battling the dark forces that constantly threatened Egypt's order and existence. These forces were led by Ra's arch rival, the great serpent, Apep—the symbol of chaos and destruction. Despite his nightly trials, Ra always emerged victorious to begin a new day. All the creatures of the earth rejoiced at the sunrise, and priests performed celebratory rituals at sun temples.

How did the Egyptian calendar come to have 365 days each year?

When Ra learned that Nut had become pregnant with Geb's children, the sun god angrily prohibited her from having the children on any day of the year. Thoth, the moon god of magic and wisdom, intervened and added five days to the calendar's existing 360. This allowed Nut a small window of time in which she gave birth to Osiris, Isis, Seth, and Nepthys.

Osiris was a god of agriculture and fertility. Egyptian mythology says he became the country's first king and was a popular, handsome, and charismatic ruler. Osiris taught his people how to farm the land, make bread and wine, and worship the gods. He built cities and established a just code of laws. Osiris took his loyal sister, Isis, goddess of love and motherhood, as his wife and queen. Isis helped her husband civilize Egypt by teaching women how to spin and weave, grind corn, and cure illnesses. Egypt prospered.

On the other hand, Seth was the god of chaos and evil. He was as bad as his siblings were good. His sister Nepthys, a goddess of the dead, became his wife.

 There is also a scientific explanation for adding five days to the year. The Egyptian year originally had 360 days because the Egyptians based their first calendar on the cycles of the moon. But about five thousand years ago, the Egyptians realized that their calendar would be more accurate if they based it on the position of the sun in the sky. This solar calendar gave them a more precise, 365-day year because it was properly synchronized to the period of time it takes the earth to make one trip around the sun.

Who killed Osiris?

Since Egypt was prospering, King Osiris decided to civilize the rest of the world. Isis ruled wisely while her husband was away.

When he returned, Seth held a celebratory banquet. During the festivities, Seth unveiled an elaborately decorated coffin he had made. Seth said he would give the magnificent box to whoever fit in it perfectly. The guests took turns climbing inside, but each was too tall, too short, too broad, or too thin. When Osiris's turn came, he fit the coffin perfectly, like Cinderella and her glass slipper. Seth had made the box to fit him. Before Osiris could climb out, Seth slammed the lid and nailed his brother inside. Then Seth flung the chest into the Nile.

With Osiris out of the way, Seth became king of Egypt. Isis, devastated, set out to search for her husband's body. Osiris's coffin had drifted all the way down the Nile and across the Mediterranean Sea. It came ashore (in present-day Lebanon) and became encircled by the trunk of a great cedar tree. Isis eventually found the great tree and took the coffin back to Egypt. There she hid the coffin in the marshes. Isis used magic to revive Osiris long enough to conceive a son, Horus.

What happened to Osiris?

Before Isis could bury Osiris's body, Seth found it in the marshes. Enraged, he cut his brother's body into many pieces and scattered them over Egypt. Isis searched the country to gather all the remains of her husband's corpse. When she had retrieved nearly all of them, Isis used magic to put the body back together again. She asked Anubis, a god of the dead, for

Temple of Isis at Philae

help embalming and wrapping the body with cloth. Osiris was the first Egyptian mummy. He went on to become a god of the underworld, where he judged the souls of the newly dead and welcomed those who had lived a good life.

Horus and Seth fought over the throne for many years. Finally an assembly of the gods gave the crown to Horus, and Seth joined Ra in the skies as god of storms and thunder. Egyptians believed the spirit of Horus dwelled inside their pharaoh while he lived, providing a link between men and gods. Pharaohs were worshipped as god-kings living on earth.

 Since Osiris had been the god of fertility and agriculture, his rebirth represented the annual renewal of the crops. His revival also seemed to prove that Egyptians could be reborn in the underworld. Egyptians mummified their dead so the deceased could live on in the Land of the Dead—a place believed to be like Egypt, only better.

CHAPTER 3

THE MEDITERRANEAN

GREECE AND ROME

An ancient theater in Delphi, Greece, built in the fourth
century B.C.E.

 ## GREECE

What was the "golden age" in Greece?

The powerful city-state of Athens was the intellectual and
cultural center of the Greek world from about 500–323 B.C.E.
During this golden age of Greece, also called the classical
period, Athens was home to an explosion of achievements. The
first democratic government was established, as were several
schools and colleges. The Greeks made more advancements in
language and the arts and sciences than any other
Mediterranean or Middle Eastern civilization before them. They
did this chiefly by approaching mathematics, philosophy,
astronomy, and medicine with an emphasis on observation and
reasoned thinking, rather than on magic or guesswork. Greek
concepts of beauty, art, politics, and the sciences spread to
many faraway cultures through trade and conquest. The Greeks'
ideas continue to influence many of the world's cultures today.

Who told the Greek myths?

The Greeks were more interested in pure entertainment than any civilization before them. Myths were recounted by traveling *rhapsodes*, or professional performers, and staged as dramas in great open-air theaters. The Greeks' familiar and powerful stories, characters, and themes have been retold for nearly three thousand years. Partly for this reason, it is often Greek myths we think of when we think of mythology.

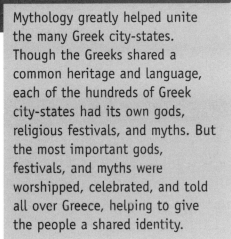

Mythology greatly helped unite the many Greek city-states. Though the Greeks shared a common heritage and language, each of the hundreds of Greek city-states had its own gods, religious festivals, and myths. But the most important gods, festivals, and myths were worshipped, celebrated, and told all over Greece, helping to give the people a shared identity.

How did the Greek gods create the universe?

They didn't; the universe created them. Gaia, who was both the earth goddess and the earth itself, emerged from a dark and formless chaos. Gaia gave birth to Uranus, the sky god and the sky itself, to blanket her completely and provide a home for future gods. Gaia also created Pontos (the sea).

Together Gaia and Uranus had many children. The first three were Hundred-handed giants, each of whom also had fifty heads. The next three children were mighty Cyclopes, giants

Our word *titanic* means massive, or having great stature or power, like the Titans. The great ocean liner *Titanic* failed to live up to its name when it tragically sank on its maiden voyage in 1912. Very successful businesspeople are sometimes called titans of industry.

who looked at the world through one enormous eye in the center of their foreheads. Uranus was so disgusted by these ugly children—and so fearful that they might one day usurp his power—that he threw them deep into the darkest, gloomiest section of the underworld.

Then Gaia and Uranus had six sons and six daughters called the Titans. The twelve Titans were also giants, but they looked like humans. Still, Uranus did not like them. Gaia was furious at Uranus for his cruelty toward his children. She urged the Titans to rise up against their father and free their siblings from the underworld. Only Cronos, the youngest and most daring, was willing to try. Cronos made a surprise attack on his father, wounding him badly with a curved knife called a sickle. Uranus fell from power, and Cronos took his place as ruler of the universe. But Cronos kept the Cyclopes and Hundred-handed giants in the underworld.

What did Cronos do to make his kids disappear? He:

a) sent them to the underworld

b) gave them a coat of invisibility

c) ate them

d) made them drink a magic potion

The answer is letter *c*. Cronos married his sister Rhea, with whom he had several children. Cronos had been warned that one of his children would someday overthrow him, just as he had overthrown his father. To avoid this fate, Cronos swallowed each of his newborn children whole. Rhea was so apalled by her husband and angry at being robbed of her children that she hatched a plan to keep her next child safe.

When Rhea gave birth to Zeus, her sixth child, she hid him on the Mediterranean island of Crete. Then she wrapped a large stone in infant's swaddling clothes and gave the bundle to Cronos. Cronos swallowed it whole.

Were Cronos's children gone forever?

Zeus grew to be a strong and swift god who was determined to rebel against his father. He married his cousin Metis, who was the daughter of a Titan and the goddess of prudence. Metis and Rhea helped Zeus gather a force to challenge Cronos and the Titans. Metis then gave Cronos a drink that she promised would make him unconquerable. Instead it made him throw up. Out came the stone Cronos had swallowed. Out came Zeus's five brothers and sisters: Demeter, Hestia, Hera, Hades, and Poseidon. The siblings banded together to take on their father and the Titans. The fighting raged for ten years before Zeus decided to free the Cyclopes and Hundred-handed giants. The Cyclopes made Zeus a thunderbolt, Hades a helmet of darkness that made him invisible, and Poseidon a *trident*, or spear, that could split the seas.

Temple of Olympian Zeus, standing in front of the Acropolis in Athens, Greece

With these new instruments of war, Zeus and his army crushed the Titans. Zeus drove all his enemies but Atlas into the underworld, where the Hundred-handed giants stood guard forever. As punishment for assuming a leading role among the Titans, Atlas was forced to take the heavens upon his shoulders and bear their weight forevermore.

Mt. Olympus is a real mountain in Greece. It's so high, and seemingly close to heaven, that the ancient Greeks thought it must be the home of the gods.

Who were the gods and goddesses of Olympus?

Zeus and the Greeks' twelve other supreme deities lived in a palace built by the Cyclopes atop Mount Olympus. Along with Zeus's five siblings were six of his children: Hephaestus, Ares, Athena, Apollo, Artemis, and Hermes. Only Aphrodite, the goddess of love and beauty, was not related to Zeus. She had no parents but sprang from the waters in a wave of foam.

Zeus married his sister Hera, the goddess of marriage and childbirth, and made her his queen. However, Zeus also married and had children with many other goddesses, Titanesses, and even mortals. Hera was always jealous of her husband's other wives, and she did not hesitate to show it.

The hierarchy of the Greek pantheon was most closely modeled on that of a human family. More than most cultures, the Greeks imagined that their gods were not so different from themselves. At their best, the gods were honest, proud, brave, resourceful, and virtuous. Yet they could also be jealous, selfish, deceptive, vain, and stubborn. Compared to the more monstrous, rigid, and irrational gods of some other cultures, Greek gods were less fearsome and more companionable.

Why was Prometheus unpopular with the gods?

Prometheus, whose name means "forethought," was a Titan who had not joined in the fight against Zeus. (Prometheus had the power to see the future and knew Zeus was going to win.)

Prometheus and his brother Epimetheus were given the task of creating animals and men. After Prometheus fashioned men and beasts out of water and clay, he let Epimetheus endow them with gifts such as speed, strength, and keen eyesight. Epimetheus, whose name means "afterthought," bestowed gifts upon the animals first. Prometheus promptly complained that nothing was left for mankind.

Rockwell Kent's *Prometheus*

Prometheus wanted to protect and provide for his creation, so he asked Zeus to at least let man have the gift of fire. Zeus refused, saying fire was only for the gods. Refusing to take no for an answer, Prometheus stole an ember from Olympus and gave it to man.

Zeus was angry to see fire on earth—but what was done, was done. As payback Zeus demanded great offerings of meat from humans. Again Prometheus stepped in to help. He told men to sacrifice an ox and separate the carcass into two piles. He then covered the meat pile with bones and entrails and topped the fur pile with a piece of juicy fat. Prometheus said Zeus could take his pick, knowing Zeus would be tricked by the fat. Zeus was enraged when he discovered what Prometheus had done. This, on top of giving man fire! To punish Prometheus, Zeus had the Titan chained to a rock, where every day an eagle pecked at him and tore out his liver. Since Prometheus was immortal, his liver grew back each night, only to be devoured again the next day.

What kind of jar could humans do without?

Still trying to punish mankind for receiving fire, Zeus ordered the creation of Pandora, the first woman. Zeus gave her a jar, warned her never to open it, and sent her to earth.

Pandora, whose name means "gift to all," dazzled men with her beauty. But she was insanely curious. *What was in the jar?* She had to know! Pandora cracked the lid and out flew old age, along with disease, lies, greed, envy, and a host of other evils. She slammed the lid shut, but it was too late. The miseries were out in the world. However, there was one good thing in Pandora's jar that humans could turn to in their distress—hope.

Why did winter come, according to the Greeks?

Demeter, the goddess of crops and the harvest, cherished her only daughter, Persephone (also called Kore, or "maiden"). Persephone was so fair and full of grace that even the somber lord of the underworld, Hades, fell in love with her. Hades wanted Persephone for his queen, but knew Demeter would never agree to the match.

One day while Persephone was gathering flowers in a meadow, the earth split open. Hades charged up from the underworld and seized Persephone. When Demeter realized that her daughter was missing, she began a frantic search. Demeter was so distraught that nothing grew on earth. People and animals starved. The gods begged her to bless the earth once more, but she refused to let anything bloom or grow until she had found Persephone.

Finally Demeter learned from one of the gods that Hades had kidnapped her daughter. Demeter appealed to Zeus, threatening to leave the earth barren forever if Persephone was not returned to her. Zeus ordered Hades to release Persephone. He told Demeter that, as long as the girl had not eaten anything in the underworld, she could come home—for once someone had consumed food or drink of the dead, that person could not return to the world of the living. But just as Persephone was ready to leave the underworld, Hades tricked her by giving her pomegranate seeds, a symbol of marriage. Because she ate four of them, Zeus decided that she could return to earth, but she would have to spend four months of the year—one month for each pomegranate seed she had eaten—as Hades's queen in the underworld. During those winter months, Demeter is so upset that the earth lies cold and fruitless. When mother and daughter are reunited in the spring, the earth becomes warm and full of life.

Who solved the riddle of the Sphinx?

Oedipus, the king of Thebes, was the son of King Laius and Queen Jocasta, though he did not know it. Before Oedipus was born, Laius consulted the Oracle at Delphi, who told him that his unborn son would one day kill him and marry Queen Jocasta. When Oedipus was born, Laius left him in the mountains to die. Oedipus was found, though, and raised by the king and queen of Corinth as their own son.

When Oedipus grew up, he visited the Oracle at Delphi himself to learn his future. The oracle told him that he would kill his father and marry his mother. Horrified, Oedipus fled Corinth so that the oracle would not come true. On a narrow road near Thebes, Oedipus met a chariot whose driver shouted, "Make

When an ancient Greek had an important decision to make, that person would consult an *oracle*. An oracle was a priest or priestess who received and translated messages from the gods. (The messages themselves were also called oracles.) The oldest and most important of these fortune-tellers was the one Heracles consulted, the Oracle of Apollo at Delphi.

way for our master's chariot!" The servants in the chariot tried to push Oedipus off the path, and he fought back. Tragically, he killed the driver, all but one of the servants, and the master—King Laius.

Oedipus continued on to Thebes, where he found the city's gates closed because of a monster called the Sphinx. The Sphinx had the head of a woman, the body of a lion, the tail of a serpent, and the wings of an eagle. She challenged anyone who wanted to enter or leave the city with a riddle; if the person could not figure out the answer, the Sphinx ate him. But Oedipus answered the riddle correctly, so enraging the Sphinx that she killed herself.

The people of Thebes were so grateful to be rid of the evil Sphinx that they made Oedipus their king. He took Queen Jocasta's hand in marriage, thereby fulfilling the rest of the oracle. Oedipus and Jocasta had many happy years together,

Can you solve the riddle of the Sphinx?

"What animal walks on four feet in the morning, two at noon, and three in the evening?"

Answer: Man, who creeps on all fours in childhood, walks upright on two legs in adulthood, and uses a cane in old age.

neither knowing of their relation, until a terrible plague fell upon Thebes. People and animals were dying, and Oedipus was desperate to stop it. Once again he consulted the oracle, which said that the plague would end once the one who had murdered Laius had been punished. Oedipus determined to find and trounce the killer. When Oedipus and Jocasta learned the truth, Jocasta took her own life. Oedipus blinded himself, preferring not to live in the light that illuminated his shame. He left Thebes and died near Athens.

Where did Orpheus go that no mortal had gone before?

Orpheus was renowned as the greatest human musician. His exquisite music awed even stones and rocks, which gathered round to listen. Orpheus loved his wife, Eurydice, so much that when she died of a snakebite, he went to the underworld in a desperate attempt to bring her back to earth. He played his lyre and sang with such feeling that even Hades was moved. When Orpheus begged for the release of his beloved Eurydice, Hades agreed, on one condition: Eurydice would follow Orpheus out of the underworld, but he must not look back at his wife until both had safely returned to the land of the living.

Orpheus immediately began to climb out of the chilly gloom of the underworld. By the time he had nearly reached the bright light of earth, he worried that Eurydice was not behind him after all. As he stepped into the light, Orpheus turned around. He saw Eurydice only long enough for her to whisper "Farewell" before she fell back into the pits of darkness. For his lack of faith, Orpheus lost his wife forever.

TRUE OR FALSE Heracles was the greatest Greek hero.

True. Heracles, the son of Zeus and the mortal princess Alkemene, was the strongest man on earth.

Heracles was not perfect. His strength and bravery were coupled with a temper so ferocious it bordered on madness. Once in a terrible fit of rage, he killed his own wife and children. When Heracles realized what he'd done, he went to an oracle and asked what he could do to redeem himself. The oracle said Heracles must go to his cousin King Eurystheus of Tiryus and perform any labors the king desired. Heracles's status as a hero soared when he completed these tasks, known as the Twelve Labors of Heracles.

What were some of Heracles's trying labors?

Heracles had to rid the countryside of four menacing beasts. Among them was the monstrous Lion of Nemea, whose hide repelled all weapons, and the nine-headed Lernaean Hydra, who grew two new heads whenever one was cut off.

For his fifth labor, Heracles was told to clean out the Augean Stables in a single day. These filthy stables, home to thousands of cattle, had not been cleaned for years and were piled high with dung. Heracles completed the dirty job, which should have taken a year, by diverting the waters of two mighty rivers to wash the stables clean.

For most of his remaining labors, Heracles had to retrieve objects and animals that were far from home and nearly impossible to obtain. One of the objects was the golden girdle,

or belt, of Hippolyta, queen of the Amazons. The Amazons were a society ruled by women warriors, whom Heracles defeated. Heracles was also told to get the golden apples of the nymph Hesperides, which were guarded by a dragon and could only be picked by a god. Heracles slew the dragon and then held up the sky while Atlas picked the apples for him. The last labor of Heracles was to capture Cerberus from his post at the gates of the underworld and parade him before King Eurystheus.

 Would the ancient Greeks recognize the Hercules of Disney's animated movie of the same name? (Hercules was the Romans' name for Heracles.) The movie accurately shows Heracles's strength and character, but it ignores the hero's labors. And it tells you that Hera is the hero's real mother and that Hades is his archenemy. These story lines, invented for the sake of the movie, would've been new to the Greeks and Romans.

How did Perseus slay the gorgon Medusa?

Perseus, the son of Zeus and a mortal woman, was commanded by King Polydectes to slay the gorgon Medusa and bring him her head. The king was secretly in love with Perseus's mother, and he hoped to get rid of Perseus; no one had ever returned from such a quest. The gorgons were three hideous female monsters who had snakes for hair. They had dragonlike scales that no weapon could pierce. Worst of all, one look from a gorgon turned a person to stone.

Hermes, the swift messenger of the gods, told Perseus that he would need some equipment owned by the nymphs of the north. They gave Perseus winged sandals, a cap that made the wearer invisible, and a pouch in which to carry Medusa's head. Hermes gave Perseus his sword, which was so strong that the gorgons' scales would not bend or break it. The goddess Athena appeared and gave Perseus the last thing he needed: her shield, polished to a high shine.

Wearing the winged sandals, Perseus flew off to find the gorgons. All around the gorgons' lair were figures of stone—figures that had once been men. Perseus used Athena's shield as a mirror to keep from looking directly at the gorgons and being turned to stone himself. He swooped down toward the gorgons

An astronomical chart showing the constellation Perseus

and sliced off Medusa's head in one swift motion. Grabbing the head by its snaky locks, Perseus threw his trophy into the magic bag and, wearing the cap of invisibility, sped away before the two other gorgons could find him.

When Perseus arrived at King Polydectes's court, he found that the king had made his mother a slave because she refused to marry him. Perseus was so angry that he gave Polydectes just what he'd asked for—Medusa's head. Perseus pulled it out of the magic bag and turned the king and his men to stone.

How did King Midas get his golden touch?

Midas, the rather dim-witted king of Phrygia, learned that the satyr Silenus had been sleeping in one of his royal rose beds. (Satyrs were men with goat's legs, a horse's tail, and pointed ears, who followed Dionysus, the god of fertility and wine.) Instead of punishing Silenus, King Midas entertained him with food and wine for ten days.

In return for this generosity, Dionysus said he would grant Midas any wish. Without thinking what would happen, Midas wished that everything he touched would turn to gold. Dionysus knew what trouble this would cause, but he granted the wish anyway.

In no time, Midas was rich. But he was also starving! For any food he tried to eat turned to gold. Terrified that he would starve to death, Midas begged Dionysus to undo the wish. Dionysus told Midas to bathe in the river Pactolus, which washed away his power and returned him to normal.

What was Jason's impossible task?

Jason was a prince of Iolcus who, as a boy, was cheated out of his throne by his greedy uncle Pelias. When Jason set out to claim his crown, he met an old, haggard woman whom he carried to the other side of a stream. There the woman revealed that she was the goddess Hera in disguise. In return for Jason's kindness, Hera promised to help him in any way she could.

When Jason presented himself to Pelias, his uncle said he must retrieve the Golden Fleece if he wanted to claim his father's kingdom. It seemed impossible. The Golden Fleece was the thick fur coat of a holy bull that hung in a sacred grove in the kingdom of Colchis. It was guarded by a never-sleeping dragon. Remembering Hera's promise, Jason accepted the challenge.

Who were the Argonauts?

Jason assembled a crew of heroes to set sail on his ship, the *Argo*. They called themselves the Argonauts. With Hera's help, they sailed across the seas to their destination. King Aeetes of Colchis was enraged that the Argonauts had landed in his kingdom. Jason told the king that they had come to offer their services in return for the Golden Fleece. The king challenged Jason's crew to harness his fire-breathing bulls to a plow and use them to sow a field with dragon's teeth. Aeetes was sure the Argonauts would die trying to complete this deadly assignment.

But Jason had Hera on his side. The goddess compelled Medea, the king's daughter and a powerful sorceress, to fall in love with Jason—so deeply that she betrayed her own father to save Jason's life. Medea concocted a magic potion to protect Jason, who then subdued the bulls and plowed the fields. As soon as Jason had planted the dragon's teeth, fierce warriors sprang out of the ground, ready to fight. Jason threw a rock among them and watched as each blamed and beat to death the others.

Yet King Aeetes still would not surrender the Fleece. While the king plotted to kill Jason and the Argonauts, Medea warned Jason. She took him to the sacred grove and cast a spell to make the never-sleeping dragon nap. Jason seized the Fleece, and he and Medea escaped on the *Argo* back to Iolcus.

Even though Jason had done the impossible, he never wore the crown of Iolcus. Upon their return to Greece, Medea tricked Pelias's daughters into killing their father in a vat of boiling water, telling them the water would make Pelias young again. The people of Iolcus were so outraged that they refused to allow

Jason to take the throne. The couple fled to Corinth, where Jason eventually died.

Which Greek hero completed an a-*maz*ing feat?

Half man and half bull, the Minotaur was a terrible flesh-eating beast that was kept by Crete's King Minos in a *labyrinth*, or winding maze. Every nine years, King Minos demanded that King Aegeus of Athens send seven young men and seven young women to be sacrificed to the Minotaur. King Aegeus's son, Theseus, volunteered to be one of the sacrifices so he could slay the Minotaur. Reluctant to let his son go, the king made Theseus promise to replace the black flag on his ship with a white one if he was returning safely to Athens. Theseus agreed.

Upon arriving in Crete, Theseus met Ariadne, the daughter of King Minos. Ariadne fell instantly in love with Theseus and determined to help him escape the labyrinth. She gave him a sword and a spool of thread. When Theseus entered the labyrinth, he tied one end of the thread to the entrance and unspooled the ball as he searched for the Minotaur. Theseus found the evil creature, killed it with the sword, and followed his string trail back to the entrance of the labyrinth. As soon as Theseus rescued all the other Athenians who'd been sent as sacrifices, he rushed them to the ship and set sail for home, leaving Ariadne behind. Theseus was in such a hurry to get away from Crete that he forgot to change the flag on his ship. When King Aegeus saw the black flag flying over his son's vessel, he was so upset that he threw himself into the sea and drowned. Theseus became king of Athens, and the waters into which King Aegeus had plunged became known as the Aegean Sea.

The myth of the labyrinth may have been inspired by the royal palace of Knossos, which was built by the Minoans, a people who lived on Crete between about 2000–1450 B.C.E. An excavation of the palace in the early twentieth century found many chambers, storerooms, courtyards, winding hallways, and paintings of bullfights.

How did Daedalus escape from King Minos?

After Theseus killed the Minotaur, King Minos was convinced that Daedalus, the skilled architect and builder of the labyrinth, had revealed the secret of the maze to Ariadne. Minos threw Daedalus and his son, Icarus, into prison.

Daedalus, who was also an inventor, secretly fashioned two pairs of wings, made of feathers fastened together with wax. When he was finished, he took Icarus to a high tower in the prison. Just before father and son took flight, Daedalus warned Icarus not to fly too close to the sun. Once in the air, though, Icarus became so exhilarated by the glory of flying that he climbed higher and higher into the sky. As he got nearer to the sun, the wax holding his wings together began to melt. The wings fell apart and Icarus plunged to his death. Daedalus, though heartbroken, flew on and landed on the island of Sicily, where he spent the rest of his life.

Why do spiders spin webs?

Athena was the goddess of spinners and embroiderers. She heard that a mortal peasant girl named Arachne was boasting that her weaving was better than the goddess's. Athena challenged Arachne to a contest, and Arachne immediately accepted.

During the contest, both spinners' hands flew in a flurry of thread and exquisite cloth. The two finished their weaving at the same time, and Athena was enraged to see that Arachne's cloth was as perfect as her own. Athena tore the cloth from Arachne's loom and beat the girl around the head with her spinning shuttle. Arachne was so disgraced by this treatment that she hanged herself. Feeling sorry for what she'd done, Athena sprinkled some magic water on Arachne's body and turned the girl into a spider, allowing her to keep her extraordinary spinning skill forever.

How did an apple start the Trojan War?

The Judgment of Paris by Enide-Rene Menard

When Eris, the goddess of discord, was not invited to the wedding of King Peleus and his sea nymph bride, Thetis, furious Eris sent to the wedding feast a golden apple inscribed with the words "To the fairest." The goddesses Hera, Athena, and Aphrodite all claimed the apple, each declaring herself to be the fairest. Zeus appointed Paris, a prince from the great walled city of Troy, to settle the dispute.

Each goddess promised to give Paris a gift if he proclaimed her the winner. Hera promised royal power. Athena offered wisdom and victory in war. And Aphrodite pledged to bring him the most beautiful woman in the world. Paris proclaimed Aphrodite to be the fairest. She fulfilled her promise by kidnapping Helen, Greek queen of the city-state Sparta, and bringing her to Troy.

But Helen was already married to King Menelaus of Sparta. When Menelaus learned what had happened to his wife, he and his brother, King Agamemnon of Argos, assembled an army of princes from all over Greece. Each prince brought his warriors, and soon a thousand ships set sail for Troy. After landing near the walled city, the Greeks attacked Troy, beginning a war that would last ten years.

What was unique about Achilles and his heel?

Achilles was the greatest Greek hero of the Trojan War. As a child, Achilles had been dipped into the River Styx by his mother, who wanted to make him indestructible. The only part of Achilles's body that remained vulnerable was the heel by which his mother had held him.

Achilles grew up to be a brave, proud, and ruthless warrior. Almost single-handedly, he forced the fighting Trojans to retreat into their walled city, felling soldiers by the dozens. The Trojan commander, Hector, remained outside the walls to challenge Achilles. The great warrior chased Hector around the city three times before killing him.

Achilles continued to fight bravely until Paris saw him—and drew his bow. With guidance from Apollo, the god of archery, the arrow struck Achilles's vulnerable heel and killed him. Today, when we talk about a crucial flaw that causes a person to fail, we call that flaw the person's "Achilles' heel."

MYTHIC VOICES:

66 . . . the rabble of routed Trojans was thankful to crowd within the city till their numbers thronged it; no longer did they dare wait for one another outside the city walls, to learn who had escaped and who were fallen in the fight, but all whose feet and knees could still carry them poured pell-mell into the town. **99**

—FROM THE *ILIAD*, TRANSLATED BY SAMUEL BUTLER

How was winning the Trojan War a "hollow victory" for the Greeks?

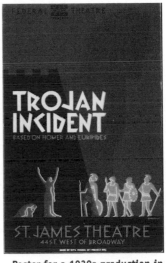

Poster for a 1930s production in New York City

Soon after Achilles's death, the Greeks boarded their ships and sailed away, leaving an enormous wooden horse outside the walls of Troy. The horse bore an inscription dedicating it to the goddess Athena. Puzzled by the presence of the horse but overjoyed to see the Greeks gone, the Trojans brought the horse into the city as a trophy and a gesture to win Athena's favor.

That night the Trojans went to their homes with a peacefulness they had not enjoyed for ten years. But their sense of well-being did not last long. The giant horse was a ploy devised by Odysseus, a Greek warrior known for his wisdom and craftiness. It was hollow and full of Greek soldiers, who climbed out while Troy slept. The soldiers opened the city's gates to the rest of the Greek army—for the ships had not sailed away, but instead had been hidden behind an island! The Greeks burned and pillaged the city and began attacking its dazed inhabitants before the Trojans could climb into their armor. The brutal and bloody battle destroyed the city of Troy and cost many lives on both sides. It also ended the war.

Although the Greeks were victorious, they still faced hardships. While sacking Troy, they'd ruined holy temples and shrines, which angered the gods. This caused the gods to stir up storms as the Greeks sailed for home, destroying much of the fleet.

Men who survived were scattered far and wide; they ended up traveling for many years through places such as Africa or Italy before reaching Greece. When the weary, long-lost soldiers did arrive in their kingdoms, they often found them in chaos.

As for Paris and Helen, Paris died in battle, but Helen survived. She returned to Sparta with Menelaus and reigned again as queen.

Why was Odysseus late for dinner?

After ten years of fighting in the Trojan War, Odysseus spent another ten years wandering through a magical world of witches and monsters, trying to get home to his wife, Penelope, and his kingdom in Ithaca.

Early in their journey, Odysseus and his men landed on an island where they found a giant Cyclops named Polyphemus. (The Cyclops of the island was unrelated to those who helped Zeus in the war against the Titans.) Polyphemus ate four Greeks before Odysseus and the rest of his men managed to blind the one-eyed giant with a hot stake and escape. On another island, the goddess Circe turned half of Odysseus's crew into pigs. With the help of the god Hermes, Odysseus forced the goddess to transform his crew back into men. Circe asked them all to stay at her palace, which they did for a year.

When the men returned to their journey, they passed the island of the Sirens. The Sirens were monsters with bodies of birds and heads of women. Their exquisite singing caused sailors to jump ship and swim to them, only to die at their hands. Odysseus

resisted the Sirens by having himself tied to the ship's mast and plugging the crew members' ears with wax so they could keep rowing.

Odysseus and his crew encountered deadly sea monsters before arriving at Thrinakia, the island of the Sun. There the men ate several of the sacred Cattle of the Sun. Zeus was so enraged that he destroyed the ship and all the men except Odysseus, who floated to the island of the goddess Calypso. But he wasn't safe there, either. Calypso kept the unwilling king of Ithaca in her cave for eight years. Finally, with the help of the goddess Athena, Odysseus made it home.

Upon arriving in Ithaca, Odysseus found his palace crowded with suitors trying to woo Penelope and gain the king's fortune. Penelope had always refused to believe Odysseus was dead, but Ithaca was without a king and Penelope was being pressured to marry again. Disguised as an old beggar by Athena, Odysseus was able to see who among his family and citizens remained loyal to him. Then, with help from his son, Telemachus, Odysseus killed the suitors and proved his identity to Penelope, his loving and faithful wife.

MYTHIC VOICES:

66'First, therefore, give me a list of the suitors, with their number, that I may learn who, and how many, they are. I can then turn the matter over in my mind, and see whether we two can fight the whole body of them ourselves, or whether we must find others to help us.'

"To this Telemachus answered, 'Father, I have always heard of your renown both in the field and in council, but the task you talk of is a very great one: I am awed at the mere thought of it; two men cannot stand against many and brave ones. There are not ten suitors only, nor twice ten, but ten many times over; you shall learn their number at once.'99

—Odysseus and Telemachus speaking in the *Odyssey*, translated by Samuel Butler

Was there really a King Odysseus and a Trojan War?

One way we know about the Trojan War today is through two epic poems by the Greek poet Homer, the *Iliad* and the *Odyssey*. The *Iliad* is an account of the final months of the Trojan War; the story is so named because Troy was also called Ilion or Ilium. The *Odyssey* relates the perilous journey of Odysseus back to Ithaca.

 WORLD OF WORDS

An *epic* is a long, serious poem that tells the story of a hero or heroes—and, in more modern times, a heroine or heroines.

While Homer's King Odysseus was a fictional character, the *Iliad* is based at least in part on a war fought between Greeks and Trojans in Troy around 1250 B.C.E. Troy was a real place, an ancient city located in present-day Turkey. No one knew if ancient Troy existed until its ruins were found by a German archaeologist named Heinrich Schliemann between 1870 and 1890. Schliemann actually found several Troys—one built on top of the other as the previous city deteriorated. The city thought to have been the scene of the Trojan War had been looted and devastated by fire.

Although Homer was one of the most famous poets in ancient Greece, we know little about him. He is thought to have lived in the eighth century B.C.E. and is presumed to have been blind. Like most poets, he was probably a rhapsode who recited poetry from memory. This makes it difficult to know how much of his stories' content Homer heard from others and how much he invented. We also don't know if Homer actually wrote down the epics, or if someone who heard him recite them wrote them down later. But we do know that his stories have fascinated people for centuries.

Rome

Was there a time when the saying "All roads lead to Rome" was more than just an expression?

Tradition says that Rome was founded in 753 B.C.E., when Latins who had settled into villages in western Italy joined together to form a city. To the north, in present-day Tuscany, Umbria, and Latium, were the Etruscans, a cultured civilization that had adopted much from the Greeks, including their gods, alphabet, clothing styles, and sports. The Etruscans, in turn, passed many of their ways on to the Romans.

By about 265 B.C.E., Romans had taken control of most of present-day Italy. Over the centuries that followed, the city of Rome became the center of the most extensive empire in the ancient world. At the height of the Roman Empire, around C.E. 100, Roman rule extended through most of Europe, including ancient Greece, into parts of the Middle East and North Africa. The Roman army built a huge network of roads to the farthest reaches of the empire—and it did seem that all roads led to Rome!

What did Romans consider to be their most important myths?

As the Roman Empire grew, its native people came into contact with numerous foreign religions, gods, and myths. Romans tended to be unimaginative in many things, but they did have a talent for adapting the best elements of other cultures to suit their own needs. Still, native Romans had their own myths, and they were most proud of these tales of heroism and the founding of their city.

 WORLD OF WORDS

If you enjoyed cereal for breakfast, you can thank Ceres, the Roman goddess of grain and the harvest. And if you've ever been awestruck by an erupting volcano, you can praise Vulcan, the Roman god of fire and metalworking.

No culture's mythology was more accepted into Roman society than the colorful gods of the Greeks. Usually the Greek gods' and goddesses' names were replaced with Roman ones, but other times the Romans borrowed both the god and the god's name. The major Greek gods adopted by the Romans include:

Greek	Roman	Greek	Roman
Cronos	Saturn	Apollo	Apollo
Zeus	Jupiter	Aphrodite	Venus
Poseidon	Neptune	Hermes	Mercury
Hades	Pluto	Artemis	Diana
Hestia	Vesta	Hephaestus	Vulcan
Hera	Juno	Demeter	Ceres
Ares	Mars	Dionysus	Bacchus
Athena	Minerva	Eros	Cupid

Who was the greatest hero of Roman mythology?

Aeneas, the son of the goddess Venus and the mortal Anchises, fought in the Trojan War against the Greeks. When the Greeks burned Troy, Aeneas took his aged father on his back and his young son in his arms. Guided by Venus, Aeneas escaped the city with a small band of followers. The group set sail in search of a new home.

The journey of Aeneas and his men was a long and treacherous one, not unlike that of Odysseus (called Ulysses by the Romans). Aeneas was sidetracked so many times that finally a prophetess stepped in and guided him to the underworld to be reunited with his father, who had died during the voyage from Troy. Anchises told his son of the future greatness of the race he was to found in an unknown land and showed him the souls of noble Romans waiting to be born. Aeneas returned to the world of the living to make this voyage to a new homeland. He and his men landed in an area called Latinium, home of the Latins, on the western coast of Italy.

Latinium's ruler, King Latinus, had been told by an oracle that his daughter, Lavinia, was destined to marry a foreign prince. So when Aeneas arrived, the king welcomed him warmly. Lavinia's mother, however, had long planned for the princess to marry a young local king named Turnus. War broke out, and eventually Aeneas killed Turnus in combat.

Peace came when Aeneas married Lavinia, uniting the Trojans and Latins as one people. The city Aeneas founded was named Lavinium, after his wife. Aeneas's son went on to found another city, Alba-Longa. Later descendants of Aeneas founded the city of Rome in Latinium.

MYTHIC VOICES:

66 Long has my soul desir'd this time and place,

To set before your sight your glorious race,

That this presaging joy may fire your mind

To seek the shores by destiny design'd. 99

—ANCHISES SPEAKING TO AENEAS IN THE *AENEID*, TRANSLATED BY JOHN DRYDEN

 A poet named Virgil invented Aeneas's adventures.

True. When the Roman leader Octavian became emperor in 27 B.C.E., he was given the name Augustus, meaning "exalted one." Augustus was a popular ruler who governed fairly and wisely, initiating a period of peace and prosperity. He reformed the government and army, increased trade, built roads, constructed majestic public buildings and temples, and supported the arts—especially poets and writers. The most famous poet in Augustan Rome was Virgil (70–19 B.C.E.), who wrote the *Aeneid*. Modeled on Homer's Greek epics, the *Iliad* and the *Odyssey*, Virgil's story of Aeneas's adventures came not from Roman mythic tradition but from his own mind. Why? Rome was thriving under Augustan rule, and its citizens were feeling patriotic. Rome needed tradition, history, and a founder for its great empire. The

Aeneid also glorified Augustus and his family by claiming that they were direct descendants of the hero Aeneas. Roman emperors began to be seen as gods. In time every Roman schoolboy could recite long passages from the *Aeneid* from memory.

Why was a wolf important to Roman mythology?

A descendant of Aeneas named Numitor ruled the city of Alba-Longa. But Numitor was overthrown by his younger brother Amulius, who killed Numitor's sons. Then he forced Numitor's daughter, Rhea Silvia, to become a Vestal Virgin, so that she would not have any children who could claim the throne.

Despite Amulius's efforts, the god Mars seduced Rhea Silvia and left her pregnant. When she gave birth to twin boys, Romulus and Remus, Amulius threw her in prison and placed the twins in a basket to float down the Tiber River. Rather than drowning or starving, the twins washed ashore downriver and were found by a she-wolf. The wolf saved the babies by letting them drink her milk as though they were her cubs. Soon the twins were discovered by a shepherd named Faustulus, who took them home and raised them as his own children.

The twins grew up to be strong, fearless warriors. They were known to steal and, on one occasion, Remus was captured. While Remus was brought before Amulius, Faustulus decided to

Sculpture of Romulus and Remus drinking from a she-wolf

tell Romulus the truth about his birth. Romulus proceeded to free Remus, kill Amulius, and restore their grandfather, Numitor, to the throne of Alba-Longa.

Instead of waiting to become rulers of Alba-Longa, the twins decided to found their own city at the place the she-wolf had discovered them. The brothers began laying out the boundaries of their city but could not agree on the exact location of their rescue. When Romulus created a boundary ditch where he thought the line should be, Remus promptly jumped over it, as if to display its worthlessness. Enraged, Romulus killed Remus and built the new city of Rome—which he named after himself—alone, and became its first ruler.

⊘ MYTHIC LINKS The brotherly rivalry in the myth of Romulus and Remus recalls the Hebrew story about Cain and Abel. These brothers were the first children of Adam and Eve, the first man and woman of the Bible. As grown men, both Cain and Abel offered sacrifices to God. God rejected Cain's gift but was pleased by Abel's. Jealous Cain took his anger out on Abel, murdering him. God punished Cain by exiling him to a life of wandering in a distant land. (In Roman mythology, Romulus escaped punishment and was quite successful: According to some stories, after ruling Rome for more than thirty years, Romulus was made a god.)

How did Rome became a republic?

Six mythical kings ruled Rome after Romulus, each extending the city's territory, influence, and greatness—except the last king, Tarquin the Proud. Tarquin was an oppressive ruler. Yet what finally undid him was not his tyrannical ways, but a crime committed by his son Sextus.

One night Sextus and his friends got to talking about their wives. The men began to debate whose wife was leading the most virtuous life. To answer this question, they decided to drop in on each woman at home to see what she was doing. The husbands were dismayed to find their wives dining leisurely or otherwise wasting time. The only wife to live up to her husband's claims was Lucretia, who was found spinning wool. Lucretia was not only dutiful but also known for her beauty and faithfulness. Sextus found Lucretia so attractive that he returned to her home alone a few nights later. Lucretia received him graciously but soon found Sextus forcing himself upon her. She refused him. Sextus threatened that if Lucretia did not let him have his way, he would kill her and one of her slaves and leave them lying together as if they had had an affair. Rather than disgrace her family in this way, Lucretia gave in to Sextus.

 WORLD OF WORDS

A *monarchy* is a nation governed by a single ruler, such as a king or emperor, who often inherits the throne for life. A *republic* is a nation in which the citizens elect representatives to govern and make laws on their behalf. The Roman republic was ruled by an elected, three-hundred-member senate; an assembly of male citizens of military age; and two consuls, or kinglike figures chosen by the senate to serve jointly for one year.

After Sextus had gone, Lucretia summoned her husband and her father and told them what had happened. Though both men tried to comfort her and convince her that she was not to blame, Lucretia plunged a knife into her heart and killed herself. She did not want any woman to point to her actions as an excuse for their own unfaithfulness.

When the people learned of Sextus's despicable act, they avenged Lucretia's honor and death by rising up against King Tarquin and overthrowing the monarchy. Rome became a republic instead, and forever after the title "king" was despised by Romans. Lucretia was not only remembered as the woman who freed Rome from tyranny; for her faithfulness, she also stood as the Roman ideal of womanhood.

CHAPTER 4

THE FAR EAST

INDIA, CHINA, AND JAPAN

Sita and Lakshman in the forest

 INDIA

What did people of the Indus Valley create before anyone else in the ancient world?

By around 2600 B.C.E., civilization had grown up around the fertile banks of the Indus River in present-day India. Archaeological findings show that the Indus civilization was peaceful and sophisticated—so sophisticated that its houses had the world's first known indoor bathrooms!

But by 1700 B.C.E., the Indus civilization had mysteriously declined. Within two hundred years, warrior nomads from central Asia, the Aryans, arrived in northern India. The Aryans gradually settled down, adopted the farming ways of the Indus people, and took over the agricultural villages of the area. Their customs and religious beliefs eventually spread over all of India and became known as the Hindu ("of the Indus") culture.

What are the *Vedas*?

The Aryans passed on their traditions in a collection of sacred songs and hymns called the *Vedas*, or "books of knowledge." The *Vedas*, composed more than three thousand years ago, are the earliest record of the Aryans' religion, gods, mythology, and customs. For a long time, the *Vedas* were considered too sacred to be put in writing. They were passed on only by word of mouth for hundreds of years. Eventually the *Vedas* were written down in the Aryan language, Sanskrit.

The gods of the *Vedas*, or Vedic gods, usually represent powers of nature, such as fire, wind, rain, and the sun. Chief among them was Indra, ruler of the gods, the most powerful of warriors and the god of war, storms, and thunder. Indra wielded deadly thunderbolts to protect the gods and mankind from evil. In time Indra and the other Vedic gods became less important than later Hindu gods.

How many main gods do Hindus worship?

a) one   b) three   c) sixty-seven

The answer could be letter *a* or letter *b*, depending on how you look at it. There are three major gods of Hinduism: Brahma, Vishnu, and Shiva. Together these gods form the Trimurti. But each of them is a different representation of one supreme force, Brahman, the spiritual energy behind all creation. Each god in the Trimurti is male but has a female counterpart.

Brahma is the Creator, the father of both gods and humans. There are many Hindu creation myths about Brahma. One says he was born from a golden egg that floated on the first waters. Brahma split the egg in two and created heaven and earth. Then he divided himself in two, forming a man and a woman. The couple came together and the first human was born. Then the woman tried to elude the man, changing into a cow. The man became a bull, and they conceived a race of cattle. Again the woman tried to elude the man by becoming a mare; he became a stallion, and horses were born. This continued until all living things had been born, all with some of Brahma in them. Brahma is often shown with four arms and four faces, one looking in each direction. Brahma's female counterpart is Sarasvati, the goddess of wisdom, learning, music, language, and the arts.

Vishnu, the Preserver or Protector, is a kind god who defends humankind from danger. Vishnu is said to have appeared on earth to combat evil nine times, each time in a different form, or *avatar*. Two of Vishnu's most recognized avatars are the hero Rama and the god Krishna. (See pages 62 and 63.) In artwork Vishnu has four arms and is blue colored. His female counterpart is Lakshmi, the goddess of prosperity and good fortune.

Shiva is the Destroyer. Though he can be quite terrifying, he can also be considered protective, kind, and helpful, because the destruction he causes through fire makes way for creation to begin again. Shiva is often depicted as a four-armed dancer within a ring of fire, the dance representing the eternal movement of the universe and the fire depicting universal creation. He has a third eye in the middle of his forehead, which can both illuminate and destroy. His neck is blue because he holds a poison in his throat that he swallowed to protect mankind. Snakes are wrapped around his arms, and he has a cobra draped over his neck. At one time, several goddesses were recognized as Shiva's female counterpart, but eventually they united as the mother goddess, Devi (see page 60).

What goes round and round in Hindu religion and mythology?

Hindus believe that the universe creates and destroys itself over and over in an endless cycle. Brahma gives birth to the world, Vishnu protects it, Shiva destroys it—only for it all to happen again. All of this takes place during a single day and night in the life of Brahma, a period of 8.64 billion years. When Brahma awakens, the world is created; when he goes to sleep, it ends.

Humans, too, are believed to be on a cyclical path. When a person dies, his or her soul (called an *atma*) is *reincarnated*, or reborn in the body of something or someone else in the next life. Who or what depends on *karma*, or actions in the previous life. If a person lived a good life, his or her soul will be reborn as a member of a higher *caste*, or class. If not, the person might be reincarnated as a member of a lower caste. (Traditional Hindu society is divided into four distinct castes, each with specific duties.) Caste is inherited from your parents and cannot be changed within your lifetime. The only way to a higher caste is through reincarnation.

Is the Hindu goddess Devi naughty or nice?

Devi represents many Hindu goddesses rolled into one. She takes many forms. Some of her avatars are gentle, while others are downright terrifying.

Parvati, graceful and patient, tamed the wild Shiva and became the perfect wife. The couple is often shown living an idyllic life with their children Ganesha, the elephant-headed god of wisdom, and Skanda, a six-headed god of war.

Durga is sometimes said to emerge from Parvati when Parvati gets angry. She is an invincible warrior goddess with eight arms in which she holds weapons given to her by the gods. Durga was created by Vishnu and Shiva to slay the terrible demon Mahisha, a buffalo who was threatening the gods' power.

Kali, who is sometimes said to spring from Durga's forehead when Durga becomes enraged, is Devi in her most terrible form—the death goddess. Kali is portrayed as having black or blue skin and at least four arms. Like Shiva, she has a third eye in the middle of her forehead. She wears a necklace of skulls, and her tongue lolls from her mouth, ever thirsty for blood. In her four hands, she holds a holy book, prayer beads, a sword, and a severed head—two symbols of life balancing two symbols of death. Kali's role is to kill demons that threaten the world, but she is known to become so drunk with blood that she herself nearly destroys the world. Like Shiva, she causes destruction that makes way for creation.

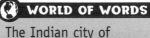
WORLD OF WORDS

The Indian city of Calcutta is said to take its name from Kali's local temple, Kali Ghat, which means "Kali's steps."

How did a fishy message save Manu from the great flood?

Manu was the first man born after Brahma divided himself in two. One day Manu was scrubbing his hands in a washbasin when he pulled up a small fish. The fish, named Matsya, begged Manu to take care of him until he was full-grown. Manu took Matsya home and put the fish in a small jar. Matsya grew quickly and had to be transferred to larger and larger containers. Finally Matsya was so big that he asked to be taken to the sea. Before he swam away, Matsya warned Manu that there would soon be a terrible flood that would consume the whole world. Matsya advised Manu to build a huge boat and to take on board seeds and living creatures of all kinds. Manu did.

Just as Manu finished his task, the rains began and the world was quickly flooded. Matsya reappeared and towed Manu's boat to the summit of a mountain that was still above water. Then Matsya revealed that he was an avatar of Vishnu. When the flood time ended, Manu showed his gratitude with a sacrifice of milk and butter. One year later, the offering turned into a beautiful woman, with whom Manu gave rise to all humankind.

Why did Vishnu come to earth as Rama?

The heroic warrior prince Rama, the seventh avatar of Vishnu, was sent to earth to defeat the ten-headed demon king, Ravana. The demon king had kidnapped Rama's wife, Sita, and taken her to the island of Lanka (today called Sri Lanka). After many trials, Rama reached Lanka, where a bloody battle ensued until Rama managed to shoot an arrow tipped with sunlight and fire into Ravana's body, killing him. Soon thereafter Rama assumed the throne of his kingdom and ruled wisely for one thousand years with Sita at his side. Even today Rama's victory over Ravana—the triumph of good over evil—is celebrated in India at the annual ten-day festival Dussehra. Twenty days later, Diwali, the festival of light, celebrates the homecoming of Rama to the city of Ayodhya, where he was crowned king. Rama's story is told in the epic the *Ramayana*, an important work of Hindu literature written around 300 B.C.E.

What is the Hindus' "great story"?

Another important Hindu epic is the *Mahabharata* ("great story"). The *Mahabharata*, whose basic story dates from 1500 B.C.E., is the longest epic in the world. (The Sanskrit composition is one hundred thousand stanzas long!)

The *Mahabharata* is the story of rivalry between two sets of royal cousins, the Pandavas and the Kauravas. The epic focuses on the five Pandava princes, who were exiled from their kingdom by the one hundred Kaurava princes. In the end, a costly eighteen-day battle results in total destruction of the Kaurava army—and eventual downfall of their family—and victory for the Pandavas.

Woven into this story line are hundreds of smaller narratives, including the *Bhagavad-Gita*, or "Song of the Lord." The *Bhagavad-Gita* is among the most sacred of Hindu texts. In it the Pandava hero prince Arjuna is overcome with grief on approaching the battlefield and seeing his opponents—his relatives. He sobs to his chariot driver, saying he cannot bring himself to fire at his relatives. The chariot driver comforts Arjuna with spiritual wisdom and urges him to do his duty as a member of the warrior class. Then he reveals his true identity as Krishna. The god's words and presence give Arjuna strength; with renewed devotion and drive, he rides into battle and leads the Pandavas to victory.

MYTHIC VOICES:

❝It was a beautiful night. The air was fresh and clean, the sky was weightless, the pyres glowed without smoke through the fine river mist. . . . Draupadi [wife of the Pandavas] and Arjuna stood alone on the battlefield all night.

In silence, resting in his embrace, Draupadi watched the sky lighten and the stars dim. . . . 'Arjuna—we are still alive!'❞

—A CONVERSATION AFTER THE BATTLE BETWEEN THE KAURAVAS AND THE PANDAVAS, FROM THE *MAHABHARATA*, RETOLD BY WILLIAM BUCK

Why does the god Ganesha have an elephant's head?

Parvati was very lonely because her husband, Shiva, was often away. So she formed their son, Ganesha, from clay while bathing in the river one day. Parvati then sent Ganesha to protect her privacy. When Shiva tried to enter the place where Parvati was bathing, Ganesha would not let him pass. Not knowing Ganesha was his son, Shiva chopped off the boy's head. Parvati, infuriated and awash with grief, demanded that Shiva replace her son's head. The first head Shiva could find was that of an elephant.

 In India the elephant has long been a symbol of strength, wisdom, loyalty, goodwill, and happiness. Wise and generous Ganesha is an extremely popular god among Hindus.

Ganesha grew up to be the gentle and kind god of wisdom and prosperity, and the patron of businesspeople. Hindus embarking on a new venture pray to Ganesha, who removes obstacles to success by clearing them away with his trunk. Ganesha has four arms and a round belly, which is stuffed with the many sorrows of the world that he swallows to keep them from afflicting humans on earth. He is often portrayed with a mouse or rat at his feet, symbolizing the camaraderie between and equal importance of creatures great and small. Ganesha has only one tusk, having broken off the other when asked by the scholar Vyasa, the author of the *Mahabharata*, to record the epic. Aware of the importance of the task, Ganesha used his tusk as a pen rather than employing an ordinary writing utensil.

China

Is China the world's oldest civilization?

Though other civilizations were established first, China is generally considered the world's oldest continuous civilization. Just as Egypt grew by the Nile, Chinese culture began alongside the Huang (Yellow) River around 3000 B.C.E. Here small farms grew into villages and later into towns and cities run by ruling families, or *dynasties*. The first recorded dynasty is the Shang, whose people developed the first form of Chinese writing, calligraphy. The Shang also cultivated silkworms and spun silk into fine cloth. This was one of China's most valuable products.

The Chinese had an innovative and technologically advanced civilization. They invented the potter's wheel, the wheelbarrow, paper, the compass, gunpowder, the greenhouse, and clocks, among other things. Their great scholars included talented astronomers who predicted eclipses, recorded the first comet sighting, and made elaborate star charts.

 The Silk Road was the trade route that first linked China to the West in about 112 B.C.E. Traders carried goods like Chinese silk and pottery west, and Roman glassware, Indian spices, and other luxury goods east. But these were not the only things traveling the rugged route. Ideas, stories, news, religion, and myths made their way across Asia as well, influencing many cultures along the way.

Where does Chinese mythology come from?

The early Chinese worshipped hundreds of gods, including those of the sun, earth, rain, mountains, rivers, and clouds. People also worshipped the spirits of their ancestors.

In the sixth century B.C.E., two philosophies, Confucianism and Taoism (also spelled Daoism), became popular. While Confucianism remained more a system of ethics than a faith, Taoism grew into a true religion—with gods, rituals, and stories.

Along with Buddhism, which came to China from India and other Asian countries between 50 B.C.E. and C.E. 50, these became the main belief systems of China. Over time people combined aspects of Confucianism, Taoism, and Buddhism with ancestor and nature worship to create a sort of Chinese popular religion. Their rich mythology and vast pantheon of gods grew out of the mix.

Recorded Chinese mythology dates back almost four thousand years, though the stories were probably told much earlier than that. Many of the myths that survive today were recorded during the Han dynasty (202 B.C.E.–C.E. 220).

 The ancient Chinese developed writing as a way to consult their gods and to seek help in making decisions about the future. People of the Shang dynasty wrote questions to their gods or ancestors on oracle bones—the shoulder blade of a pig or ox, or the shell of a turtle. A priest applied a hot metal rod to the bone until the bone cracked, then interpreted the cracks as replies from the gods.

What are the main ideas of Confucianism, Taoism, and Buddhism?

Confucianism began as a political philosophy founded by Kong Fuzi (Confucius), a teacher and philosopher who lived in China from 551-479 B.C.E. Confucius spent his life inspiring people to do good and to respect and live in harmony with others. He said the peacefulness and well-being of society depended on duty to, and respect for, those above you in the social order: Children deferred to parents, wives to husbands, citizens to rulers, and rulers to gods. All Chinese emperors, whose combined rule spanned two thousand years, followed the teachings of Confucius.

Partly in response to Confucianism, a philosophy called Taoism developed. Taoism is thought to be based upon the teachings of Lao Tzu (b. 604 B.C.E.). Taoists believe that the movement and behavior of everything in the universe is governed by a single natural order, and is balanced between the opposite forces of

Yin and Yang. Taoists seek to live in selfless harmony with others and the natural world by following the spiritual path called *Tao* ("The Way").

Buddhism was founded by a minor Indian prince named Siddhartha Gautama, who lived during the sixth century B.C.E. At age twenty-nine, Siddhartha dedicated himself to seeking the true meaning of life and an end to people's pain. After six years of meditation, he sat under a bodhi tree; forty-nine days later, he found the answers he'd been searching for. He became known as the Buddha, or "enlightened one," and spent the rest of his life teaching others his ideas: that all human life is suffering caused by desire for people, pleasure, and objects, all of which are impermanent. Humans are born over and over again until they learn to conquer this desire.

What's the Chinese recipe for creating the universe?

In the beginning, there was nothing but darkness and an egg-shaped chaos. The egg was produced by the mingling of Yin and Yang, the two opposing forces of the universe. (Yin is the representation of the female—dark, soft, and cold—while Yang represents the male—light, hard, and warm.) In the darkness of the egg, a god named Pan Gu was born. He grew inside the egg

As seen in the *taiji*, a symbolic representation of the Taoist forces Yin and Yang, each element includes some of the other; that's how the two relate. The taiji shows that the forces are equally important and equally dependent upon each other.

for eighteen thousand years, until the egg burst open. The light parts of the egg, Yang, floated upward and became the heavens; the heavier parts, Yin, sank down and became the earth. To keep the earth and sky separate, Pan Gu stood on the earth, held the heavens on his shoulders, and grew ten feet every day. He did this for another eighteen thousand years, until heaven and earth were fixed in their present positions. Then weary Pan Gu lay down and died. His breath became wind and clouds. His voice became thunder, his blood rivers, lakes, and oceans. His right eye became the moon; his left, the sun. The rest of Pan Gu's body became the other parts of the universe: stars, mountains, trees, plants, precious metals, and rocks. His sweat fell from the sky as rain and coated the grass as dew. So Pan Gu, who arose from the interaction between opposites, both created and became the universe and everything in it.

What happened when the goddess Nu Wa became lonely? She:

a) got a pet

b) created humans

c) had a party and invited all the other gods

The answer is letter *b*. Nu Wa was one of the first goddesses to arrive on earth after Pan Gu separated earth from heaven. While gazing at her reflection in a pool, lonely Nu Wa felt that something was missing from the world. Suddenly she had an idea. She scooped up a handful of mud and molded it into a miniature copy of herself. When Nu Wa set the figure on the ground, it came to life and began to dance around with joy. It was the first human. Thrilled with her creation, Nu Wa made more. She decided to populate the whole world with people.

Eventually Nu Wa realized she needed to work more quickly. She dipped a cord into the mud and flicked it in the air. Each piece of mud became a human as it landed on the ground. (Some stories say that the people Nu Wa sculpted with her own hands were the nobles, while the mud-flicked people were the commoners.) Though the humans went off into the countryside, the goddess was never lonely again because she could hear their voices. When Nu Wa had finished creating humans, she taught them to raise children.

How did Nu Wa save her people?

Gong Gong, the god of water, and Zhu Rong, the god of fire, both wanted control of the universe. Gong Gong attacked Zhu Rong, and their battle raged out of heaven and toppled onto earth. After days of bitter fighting, Zhu Rong channeled his heat and managed to melt and burn Gong Gong's army of sea creatures. Gong Gong was so angry and ashamed that he rammed his head into Imperfect Mountain, a peak that held up one corner of the heavens. Little happened to Gong Gong's head—he was immortal, after all—but the mountain began to tremble, quake, and crumble down around him. A gaping hole opened in the sky. Rocks gashed the ground. Flames leaped and torrents of water

When the earth was thrown off balance because of the collapse of Imperfect Mountain, the world was said to tilt toward the east. This was supposed to be the reason all China's rivers flow from west to east. It was also an explanation of why the earth is tilted—something most other ancient peoples weren't even aware of. (Our planet sits at a natural angle as it travels around the sun, which is the reason we have seasons.)

gushed from deep within the earth. The whole world was thrown off balance. Terrified people screamed and ran wildly in every direction.

Nu Wa could not stand by and watch her people suffer. She gathered rocks from a riverbed and smelted them until they could be molded to fit the hole in the sky. To ensure that the heavens would not fall down again, Nu Wa took the legs of a giant tortoise (a symbol of strength and permanence) and used them to support the heavens. Then she burned some reeds and used the ashes to close up the cracks in the earth. Thus the Chinese worshipped Nu Wa as both their creator and protector.

How did Yu end a great flood?

For thirteen years, a man named Yu labored to control the waters of a great flood. The waters were so overwhelming that the people worried they would have to become fish or perish. Instead of trying to dam up the waters, Yu dug canals and rivers to direct the water into the sea. Day after day, Yu toiled. His hands and feet became so callused that he could barely hobble along; his skin became black from the sun. He grew thinner and weaker as each day passed, but still he continued to work.

Finally Yu's labors paid off. The flood waters ran into the oceans. Not only that, the canals he'd built doubled as a valuable irrigation system. Yu became a hero who was revered for his strength and dedication to hard work. The emperor was so grateful that he stepped down and gave Yu the throne.

Yu became the mythical founder of the Chinese Xia dynasty and is said to have ruled from 2205 to 2197 B.C.E. All succeeding emperors were considered to be incarnations of Yu, and were thus believed to rule with heaven's approval. The official symbol of the emperor of China is the dragon because, in early mythology, the hero Yu was depicted as a dragon or as half dragon, half human.

Dragons are among the most magical and misunderstood mythological creatures. Unlike the ugly, feared dragons in Western mythologies, who devour humans and hoard treasure (see page 115), Eastern dragons are beautiful and respected. They were worshipped as rulers of rain, rivers, lakes, and seas. Though they could cause storms, floods, or droughts when not paid proper respect, Eastern dragons were usually gentle, benevolent, and wise. They breathed clouds, not fire, and swam but did not fly.

Chinese dragons can change shape and size at will, shrinking to the size of a silkworm or expanding to fill the space between heaven and earth. They have the head of a camel, the horns of a deer, the scales of a fish, the belly of a clam, the claws of an eagle, the eyes of a bull, the ears of an ox, and the paws of a tiger. The imperial dragon, representing the Chinese empire, has five toes to distinguish it from the more common three- or four-toed dragons.

Chinese dragon statue at the Summer Palace in Peking, China

TRUE OR FALSE There is a Chinese god of examinations.

True! Due in part to the teachings of Confucius, Chinese society had a rigid, pyramidlike structure. The emperor presided over a vast system of judges, courts, and officials. The Han dynasty set up an Imperial Examination System in order to establish a fair civil service, managed by people who worked for the government, based on merit rather than on status, wealth, or privilege. Any man could enter and rise through the ranks by passing certain exams—after appealing to the god of examinations for wisdom and luck, of course! There were also gods for every profession, most of whom, like the god of examinations, were depicted in human form.

A similar kind of order characterized Chinese heaven and hell. There were mythical emperors of each who ruled over many government departments and courts that were run by lesser gods. Divine officials faced performance-based demotions and promotions, just as humans did on earth. The Jade Emperor, supreme ruler of heaven, held a position in heaven parallel to that of the Chinese emperor on earth. The two rulers were said to be in direct contact.

Where did the first silkworm come from?

Long ago a man and his daughter lived alone with their horse. The father had to go away on business, and his daughter missed him terribly. While she was grooming the horse, the daughter spoke to the animal and said that she would marry anyone who brought her father home. The horse immediately ran off.

When the horse found the father working far away, he began to neigh and act as though something were wrong. Worried, the man climbed onto the horse's back and returned home. The daughter was overjoyed to see her father. She told him that the horse must have known how much she had missed him. The father rewarded the horse with extra food, but the animal would not eat. The horse behaved strangely except when the daughter was around, when he whinnied with excitement. Wondering what was causing the odd behavior, the father asked his daughter if she knew anything about it. She remembered what she'd said about marriage and told him. Enraged that an animal would even think about marrying his daughter, the father killed the horse, skinned it, and hung the hide out to dry.

The next day the skin flew off the line, wrapped itself around the daughter, and carried her away. The father chased the hide into the woods and finally found his daughter, still wrapped in the skin, high in a mulberry tree. The girl had turned into a caterpillarlike creature. Her horse-shaped head bobbed up and down, spinning a thin white thread that she wrapped around herself. The daughter had become the first silkworm. Her thread was so strong and beautiful that it was used to make clothes for the emperors.

JAPAN

Where did Japan's first settlers come from?

Japan's first inhabitants started arriving from mainland Asia—
China and Korea—at least ten thousand years ago and lived in
tribal groups. But it was not until the Yamato clan conquered
many neighboring clans around C.E. 500 that Japan began
moving toward a unified state, and a unified mythology. Within
a century, the Yamato prince Shotoku had taken over most of
present-day Japan and adopted many aspects of Chinese religion
and culture that had been introduced by immigrants. Today's
Japanese leaders trace their ancestry to the Yamato.

What is Shinto?

Shinto, meaning "way of the gods," is the ancient religion of
Japan and the main source of Japanese mythology. Shinto
focuses on the worship of *kami*, or gods and spirits that inhabit
the sun, moon, wind, rain, ocean, mountains, fire, animals, and
human ancestors. Traditionally
there are millions of kami. The
spirits are believed to control the
weather and seasons as well as
human life.

Early traces of Shinto beliefs and
practices date from C.E. 300.
Since then Shinto has been
influenced by Confucianism and,
especially, Buddhism. It is
difficult to separate native
Japanese beliefs from those
brought from China because
nothing about Shinto was
written down until after the
arrival of Buddhist missionaries
in 552.

Buddha statue in Kamakura, Japan

Majestic and awesome Mount Fuji, the extinct volcano near Tokyo and Japan's highest mountain, has been honored as a holy place since the first people came to the islands. Mount Fuji's spirit was said to embody and protect the nation. Today hundreds of thousands of people climb Fuji's 12,388 feet (3,776 meters) of holy ground every year.

A print of Mount Fuji and Suruga Bay by Hiroshige Andō

What is the *Kojiki*?

The earliest surviving record of Japanese history is a combination of fact and Shinto mythology called the *Kojiki*, or Record of Ancient Matters. Compiled by a member of the royal court at the request of the Japanese empress in 712, the *Kojiki* describes the creation of the world and the divine ancestry of the imperial family. Another source of Japanese myth is *Nihongi*, or Chronicles of Japan, compiled around 720.

Where did the eight islands of Japan come from?

According to the *Kojiki*, the world was an oily sea of chaos with only a formless mass "drifting like a jellyfish" upon it until a slender reed appeared between heaven and earth. This was Kuntiokatachi, the first god. Another two gods arrived, and together the three gods created seven more pairs, or generations, of deities. The last pair were the god Izanagi and the goddess Izanami, the first Japanese couple. Together Izanagi and Izanami created an island, the world's first land, and went to live there.

In order to create more islands, Izanagi and Izanami decided to have children. Soon Izanami gave birth to a son, whom they discovered was deformed. The couple named the baby Hiruko ("Leech-Child") and, with heavy hearts, set him adrift in a reed boat. Hiruko became the god of fishermen. Determined to produce healthy children, Izanagi and Izanami tried again, and Izanami gave birth to the eight islands of Japan. To beautify the islands, Izanagi and Izanami had more children: These kami were gods of trees, mountains, wind, and rivers. But when Izanami gave birth to Kagusutchi, the god of fire, she was so badly burned that she died.

MYTHIC VOICES:

❝At this time the heavenly deities, all with one command, said to the two deities Izanagi and Izanami:

"'Complete and solidify this drifting land!'

"Giving them the Heavenly Jeweled Spear, they entrusted the mission to them.

"Thereupon, the two deities stood on the Heavenly Floating Bridge and, lowering the jeweled spear, stirred with it. They stirred the brine with a churning-churning sound; and when they lifted up [the spear] again, the brine dripping down from the tip of the spear piled up and became an island. This was the island of Onogoro.

"Descending from the heavens to this island, they erected a heavenly pillar and a spacious palace.❞

—FROM THE *KOJIKI*, TRANSLATED BY DONALD PHILIPPI

 The Bridge of Heaven, upon which Izanagi and Izanami stood to churn the sea of chaos, was said to have linked the kami of heaven and those of earth. The gods could move back and forth between the worlds until the bridge collapsed into the sea—and became the *isthmus*, or narrow strip of land, that today stretches across a section of Japan's Wakasa Bay. This isthmus is called Amanohashidate, which means "Bridge of Heaven" in Japanese.

Why did Izanagi go to the underworld?

Izanagi killed his son Kagusutchi for causing Izanami's death. He then headed for Yomi, the land of the dead. From the edge of the dark land, Izanagi called out to his wife and begged her to come back to earth with him. Izanami had eaten the food of the dead, which bound her to stay in the underworld. But she told Izanagi she would ask the gods of Yomi to make an exception. She also warned her husband not to look at her.

Izanagi, impatient to see his beloved wife again, ventured into Yomi to find her. When he did, he was horrified to see that she was no longer the beautiful woman he had known but a rotting body covered with maggots. Izanami was enraged that her husband had betrayed her wishes. She and the demon spirits of the underworld chased Izanagi back to the edge of Yomi. When Izanagi reached the gate with Izanami on his heels, he turned and hurled peaches at his pursuers. Then he rolled an enormous boulder across the entrance to the underworld—an immovable barrier between life and death that still exists today.

Speaking on either side of the boulder, Izanagi and Izanami declared their marriage over. To purify himself from his trip to the underworld, Izanagi bathed in a clear stream. As he cleansed his face of the rot of Yomi, three new deities were created. When he wiped his right eye, Amaterasu, the sun goddess, was born. From his left eye came Tsuki-Yomi, the moon god. And from Izanagi's nose arose Susanowo, the storm god.

◎ MYTHIC LINKS The story of Izanagi and Izanami in the underworld is similar to the Greek myths of Demeter and Persephone and of Orpheus and Eurydice. Scholars do not agree on whether the Greek myths came to Japan, perhaps by way of trade and the spread of Buddhism, or if the myths are alike because humans naturally tend to tell the same types of stories.

Why did Amaterasu hide in a cave?

Izanagi was so pleased with his new children that he decided to divide the world among them. To Amaterasu he gave command of the High Plains of Heaven; to Tsuki-Yomi he assigned rule of the night; and to Susanowo, he bestowed control of the oceans. Amaterasu and Tsuki-Yomi accepted their assignments dutifully. But Susanowo wept and howled that he did not want to watch over the oceans; he would rather be in Yomi. Infuriated, Izanagi banished Susanowo from his kingdom.

Claiming that he wanted to say good-bye to his sister, Susanowo went to heaven. Fearing her brother's true intention was to challenge her rule there, Amaterasu armed herself. But Susanowo merely proposed a contest: Whoever could create more gods and goddesses would prove to be mightier. The sun goddess asked for her brother's sword, which she broke into three pieces, chewed up, and spit out as three beautiful goddesses. Susanowo then asked for his sister's necklace, which he used to create five gods.

When Susanowo proclaimed himself the victor, Amaterasu countered that she was the winner because the gods he'd made had come from her possession. Susanowo refused to concede. He celebrated his triumph by trampling rice paddies and blocking irrigation ditches. Then he skinned a pony and hurled it through the roof of the weaving hall where Amaterasu and her maidens were making clothing for the gods. Amaterasu was so terrified that she fled and hid herself in a cave. The sun goddess blocked the entrance with a huge boulder and refused to come out.

How did the gods lure Amaterasu out of her cave?

Without the sun goddess, heaven and earth were plunged into darkness and were subject to all manner of calamities. Crops could not grow. Chaos descended.

The gods knew they must take the matter into their own hands. Some eight hundred of them came together to discuss ways to coax Amaterasu from her cave. Finally they hatched a plan.

First the gods placed a magical mirror just outside the entrance to the cave. Then they persuaded several roosters to crow like crazy, as if it were dawn. While some gods played music, Uzume, the goddess of mirth, climbed atop a barrel and started to dance wildly. Uzume shimmied and stomped in such an outrageous way that the gods began to laugh uproariously. The ground shook as though an earthquake had struck. Amaterasu could hear all the commotion, and curiosity got the best of her. As the gods intended, Amaterasu rolled back the boulder slightly to ask what was going on. The gods replied that they were celebrating because they had found a goddess even more radiant than she. Catching a glimpse of her reflection in the mirror, Amaterasu came out of the cave to get a closer look. One god swiftly strung a rope across the cave entrance so that she could not reenter. The sun goddess was back, and things soon returned to normal.

However, Susanowo did not escape punishment for having caused this crisis. For his misbehavior and willful destruction, the gods threw Susanowo out of heaven—though he's still causing storms and mischief on earth.

The disappearance of the sun in the myth of Amaterasu and the cave is thought to be an ancient explanation of an actual event. Some scholars believe the event was a solar eclipse, when the sun's disappearance behind the moon frightened those who did not know whether the sun would reappear. Others think the myth reflects the darker days of winter and the eventual return of spring.

Where did day and night come from?

Tsuki-Yomi, the moon god, lived in heaven with his sister, Amaterasu. She sent him to visit Uke Mochi, the food goddess. Uke Mochi invited Tsuki-Yomi to stay for a meal, and then served a feast she produced from her mouth and nose. Tsuki-Yomi was so disgusted and insulted by this gesture that he killed the food goddess. From Uke Mochi's dead body arose the crops the Japanese still sow—rice, millet, wheat, and beans. Amaterasu gave these to humankind.

But Amaterasu was so angry at her brother for what he had done that she refused to see Tsuki-Yomi ever again. This is why the moon and sun are never in the sky at the same time—and thus why day and night exist.

In later versions of this myth, including the one recounted in the *Kojiki*, it is Susanowo who kills the food goddess. Scholars think that the compiler of the *Kojiki* blamed Susanowo for Uke Mochi's death to emphasize the storm god's violent nature.

Why do disease and misfortune exist?

According to Shinto belief, famine, disease, and all sorts of other miseries are caused by terrible horned demons called *oni*. Most oni are invisible, though some are thought to have the ability to appear in human or animal form. Oni are present both on earth and in Jigoku, the underworld to which sinners go when they die; oni can torment not only the living but the souls of the dead as well. They are said to have come to Japan from China, along with the arrival of Buddhism.

Those condemned to Jigoku must face a mirror in which all their past sins are reflected. The ruler of Jigoku, Emma-ho, judges male souls and assigns them to one of sixteen realms—eight of fire and eight of ice—depending on the person's earthly crimes. Female souls are judged by Emma-ho's sister. Souls can be saved only by the intervention of a *bosatsu*, or an incarnation of the Buddha.

TRUE OR FALSE **Present-day Japanese worship their emperor as a god.**

False, though this has only been the case since 1946. The Japanese traditionally believed their emperor was divine, descended from Ninigi, one of Amaterasu's grandchildren. The imperial family claimed its right to rule Japan because its members were descended from the sun goddess. In 1946, after Japan's defeat in World War II, Emperor Hirohito formally renounced his divinity before the Japanese people. Since then a prime minister has governed the nation instead of the emperor, but the emperor continues to be greatly respected by the Japanese people as a symbol of their nation.

CHAPTER 5

THE SOUTH PACIFIC

AUSTRALIA AND OCEANIA

Warlukurlangu Jukurrpa (Fire Country Dreaming)
by Rosie Nangala Flemming

 AUSTRALIA

Who are the Aborigines?

The Aborigines are the native peoples of Australia, who came by boat from Asia at least fifty thousand years ago. The Aborigines' way of life remained relatively unchanged until 1788, when the first European settlers arrived. Traditionally Aborigines were hunter-gatherers who were closely linked to the natural world. The land gave them not only water to drink and plants and game to eat, but also spiritual comfort.

The Aborigines lived in more than two thousand tribal groups made up of clans of several families. While the tribes had some interaction, they spoke different languages and told different myths (although some characters appear in the myths of more than one clan). Today about two-thirds of Aborigines have assimilated into white culture. They live and work in cities or on farms in the Australian Outback, the dry grasslands and desert in the middle of the continent. A few Aborigines continue to live much the same way their ancestors did.

What is the Dreamtime?

The Aborigines believe the world was formed by their spirit ancestors in the Dreamtime (or the Dreaming), the time of creation. The Dreamtime was an era before living memory, when the ancestors woke from their sleep and wandered through the world creating mountains, rivers, trees, plants, and animals. Some ancestors traveled in human form; others took the shape of creatures such as lizards, birds, or kangaroos. When the Dreamtime spirits finished creating, they were absorbed into the landscape and returned to sleep.

 The Dreamtime spirits also made humans.

True. In their wanderings, the Dreamtime spirits came upon shapeless bundles of plants and animals, which they began to carve with stone knives. They cut arms, legs, and faces into the bundles, creating the first human beings. Every human is linked to the plant or animal from which he or she was carved; this plant or animal is the person's *totem*. In some Aboriginal myths, humans are depicted as their totem animal.

Traditionally a newborn child's totem was determined by which ancestral spirits existed where the child was born. Each clan honored its own totems, which helped to unify clans and keep their members in touch with nature and the Dreamtime ancestors. Clan members identified with the powerful and positive qualities of their totem and avoided eating their totemic plants or animals.

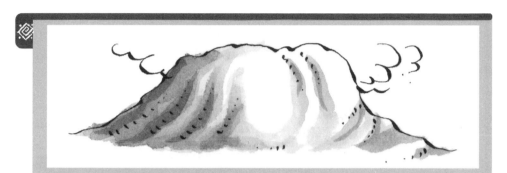

The Aborigines have a close, harmonious relationship with the natural world because the spirits of their ancestors are said to live within everything. Many rocks, streams, and caves are considered sacred and infused with the ancestors' creative energy. One of the most famous and holy sites is Uluru (also called Ayer's Rock), a massive rock that rises out of the desert and is the location of many mythical stories. At one and a half miles wide and more than a thousand feet high, Uluru is the largest single rock in the world.

How are Aboriginal myths passed on?

Their myths are passed on by storytelling, including songs or song cycles that can run hundreds of verses long. These songs are usually performed during a ceremony or ritual celebration, such as a funeral or an initiation into adulthood. Plays and dances that interpret myths may also be part of these occasions. Though the Dreamtime is an era in the distant past, it becomes part of the present; the singers, players, and dancers briefly become the ancestors whose journeys they are reliving.

Aboriginal myths are also passed on through rock, sand, bark, and body paintings. In northern Australia, Aborigines retouch cave paintings of Dreamtime spirits every year to renew the protection offered by the spirits. Many of the stories we know today were recorded by outsiders who were studying or became friends with Aborigines in the late 1800s and 1900s.

Why do all creatures die?

In the beginning, the creatures made by the Dreamtime spirits were given the ability to resurrect themselves after they died. This power did not last long, however. The first person to die was a man named Widjingara, who was killed in a battle. Widjingara's wife, Black-headed Python, wrapped her husband's body in a bark coffin and placed it on a burial platform. Then she began to mourn. She displayed her grief by shaving off all her hair and rubbing ashes all over her body, thus founding a traditional Aboriginal mourning ritual that is still practiced today.

Because Widjingara was able to revive himself, he soon returned to his wife. He was shocked to find Black-headed Python not at all welcoming. "Why have you come back?" she shrieked. "Look at what I have done to myself because of your death—my hair is gone and I am black with ashes!" Widjingara was so hurt by this hostility that he returned to his grave. Going forward, no other creature could restore himself or herself to life.

When is a snake a rainbow?

One of the most important and powerful ancestor spirits in Aboriginal mythology is the Rainbow Serpent. This snake is associated with both sky and water, and is said to live deep within lakes, rivers, and pools. When angered, the serpent takes to the sky and causes storms and terrible floods. As the serpent calms down and the storms end, a rainbow forms in the sky.

Aboriginal tribes have different names for and stories about the Rainbow Serpent. The Yolngu Aborigines of Arnhem Land, in northern Australia, call the snake Yurlunggur. The Yolngu say that two Dreamtime spirits, the Wawilak sisters, sang and danced in a frantic attempt to drive Yurlunggur away during a storm. But he swallowed them and their infant sons before rising above the floodwaters into the sky.

When the flood subsided, Yurlunggur returned to earth and spit out the sisters and their sons. The boys became the first adult

Yolngu males. Today, this myth is reenacted through song and movement during initiation ceremonies for young Yolngu men. Part of the symbolism of the event and myth is that the boys are dying and being reborn as adults when they are regurgitated by the serpent.

Were Crow's feathers always black?

In the days when Crow was still the color of snow, he made a deal with his friend Eagle. "If you fly to the hills and hunt for kangaroo, I will go to the lake in pursuit of ducks. Whatever we catch, we will share with each other at the end of the day." Eagle agreed and set off for the hills. Crow went down to the lake and, using a long hollow reed as a snorkel, lurked beneath the waters. When ducks swam by, Crow pulled them under.

When he was satisfied with the extent of his kill, Crow cooked the ducks over an open fire, ate them, and then returned empty-handed to Eagle, who hadn't caught a single kangaroo. Crow did this for several days. Finally Eagle became suspicious. Returning from the hills early one day, Eagle found Crow desperately trying to hide the remains of his recent meal. Sharp-eyed Eagle spotted grease on the fire and around the edges of Crow's mouth. Angered and humiliated, Eagle pushed Crow into the ashes again and again until Crow was completely black, as he has been ever since.

 ## Oceania

Is there one mythology of Oceania?

There are more than twenty-five thousand islands in the South
Pacific, many of them tiny. Oceania is home to many different,
small, often isolated communities. This makes for a great
diversity among the region's peoples, cultures, languages, and
stories. But while there are hundreds of mythologies, common
subjects do exist. These include stories of trickster heroes; great
sea voyages and the seafaring way of life; how the islands and
the ocean came to be; and the arrival of strangers from the sea.
Traditionally these myths have been passed on orally, often
through song and ritual. Much of what we know about Oceanic
mythology was recorded by European missionaries in the 1800s.

Why are land and sea at odds in Polynesia?

The Maori (natives of New Zealand) and other Polynesians
believe that in the beginning of the world, the creator gods
Papa, the earth mother, and Rangi, the sky father, were locked
in an embrace. Their six children were trapped between them
and desperate to escape. Tu, the war god, suggested killing their
parents to achieve this goal. But Tane, the god of forests, said it
would be better to push their parents apart. Agreeing it was
worth a try, each sibling made an effort to separate Papa and

Rangi. Haumia, the god of wild plants, and Rongo, the god of cultivated plants, failed, as did Tangaroa, the god of the sea and fishes. Tu had no luck, nor did Tawhiri, the god of wind and other elements. Only Tane was left. He put his feet against Papa and his head against Rangi and pushed with all his might. Slowly, earth and sky separated and assumed their present positions.

Instead of celebrating Tane's victory, his siblings grew jealous and turned against him. Tangaroa called the fish, who used to live on Tane's land, into the sea. Ever since Tangaroa and Tane have been at war: The sea tries to overwhelm the land with floods, while the land provides wood for canoes so that people can tame and sail upon the sea.

> **⊘ MYTHIC LINKS**   Tane's use of his body to push earth and sky apart and fix them in their present positions is reminiscent of the same feat accomplished by China's Pan Gu. The Chinese myth could have traveled to Polynesia with Southeast Asian settlers, some of whose ancestors had come from or traded with China.

Who created the first Polynesian people?

When Tane wanted a wife, he molded a woman out of clay and breathed life into her. She was called Hine. The children of Hine and Tane were the first Polynesian people. One of the daughters was named Hine like her mother. Tane took this daughter as his second wife. When the girl learned that Tane was her father, however, she fled in horror to the underworld. There she became the death goddess Hine-Nui-Te-Po.

What did Maui do for humans?

Maui, a powerful Polynesian hero and trickster, is perhaps the best-known character in Oceanic mythology. Maui created the islands of Polynesia while fishing in a canoe. The hero felt a great tug on his line, which seemed to come from such a gigantic fish that he used superhuman strength to pull it in. To his surprise, Maui realized he had no fish at all but an entire island—a place for humans to live. Some stories say that the land Maui pulled up was Te-ika-a-Maui, or the Fish of Maui, the North Island of New Zealand. (If you look at the map on page 9, you'll see that the head of the fish faces south and its tail stretches to the north.)

Maui also brought humans the secret of fire from the underworld. He did this by tricking the fire-keeper, Mahui-ike, into giving up her fingernails, which burned with the source of fire. Mahui-ike threw the last fingernail onto the ground, igniting a blaze. Maui asked the rain to come and extinguish it. But before the rain could finish its job, Mahui-ike threw a few sparks into the trees. From then on, humans knew they could use wood to build a fire.

What was Maui's version of daylight saving time?

Maui's mother complained that the sun sped by so quickly that she did not have enough hours in the day to make tapa (bark cloth) or cook meals. So cunning Maui went to the highest peak on the Hawaiian island that is named for him and waited for the sun to speed by. When it did, Maui lassoed it and held on tight until the sun agreed to travel at a slower pace, giving all living things more hours of daylight.

Did Maui always win?

Maui made a bold attempt to gain immortality for humans. He traveled to the underworld with his friends, the birds. Together they came upon the enormous death goddess, Hine-Nui-Te-Po. The goddess was sleeping, and Maui was certain that if he climbed into her body and came out her mouth, he would win immortality. Just before he crept inside Hine-Nui-Te-Po's body, Maui warned his friends not to laugh. But one bird found the sight so comical that he began to laugh hysterically. The sound woke the giant goddess, who squeezed her insides together and crushed Maui, killing him. Since Maui was unsuccessful, humans cannot escape death.

 WORLD OF WORDS

The English word *taboo* comes from the Polynesians. They first used the word *tabu* to refer to something that was too holy or powerful to touch, do, or mention—for fear of inviting the rage or disfavor of the gods. It was tabu, for example, to call after a fisherman and ask where he was going, or he would not catch anything. Other rules of tabu were significant enough to take the place of laws.

Where does the goddess Pele live?

a) in a volcano   b) on the beach

c) in the sky

The answer is letter *a*. According to Polynesian mythology, the volcano goddess Pele makes her home in Mount Kilaueau, on the island of Hawaii. Mount Kilaueau is one of the most active volcanoes on earth. It is said that the volcano's eruptions are caused by Pele's frequent tantrums.

Pele once traveled in spirit form to the island of Kauai, where she fell in love with a local chief named Lohiau. Before long Pele's spirit had to return to her body on Hawaii. But Pele sent her younger sister, Hi'iaka, to find Lohiau and lure him to Mount Kilaueau. Pele made Hi'iaka promise that she would not encourage Lohiau if he became attracted to her. In return Pele said she would not let her destructive lava flow over a grove of trees where Hi'iaka liked to dance.

After Hi'iaka had been gone for some time, Pele grew suspicious. She unleashed a flood of lava down the mountain and into the special grove. When she found the couple was back in Hawaii, she tried to kill Hi'iaka and Lohiau with another explosive stream of lava. Lohiau, a mortal, died, but the goddess Hi'iaka did not. However, Hi'iaka found Lohiau's spirit and reunited it with his body, bringing the chief back to life. Hi'iaka and Lohiau then fled to Kauai and lived happily together until Lohiau died a natural death. Pele continued her tempestuous ways, hurling lava at anyone, friend or foe, who provoked her temper.

The volcano goddess Pele is both feared and revered for her awesome power. Volcanoes are dangerous and destructive, to be sure. But they also have the power to create. Scientists think the Hawaiian Islands were produced by the eruption of undersea volcanoes, which spewed hot liquid rock from deep within the earth. When the rock cooled and hardened, it became land. So without volcanoes, Hawaii probably wouldn't exist!

CHAPTER 6

AFRICA

SUB-SAHARAN AFRICA

**Wooden mask of a spirit of the underworld,
from the Ibibio tribe**

 AFRICA

Why are there so many different cultures in sub-Saharan Africa?

South of the Sahara Desert, which dominates the northern
quarter of the continent, Africa is full of tropical grasslands, rain
forests, and jungles. These varied climates and landscapes,
along with huge lakes and rivers full of rapids and waterfalls,
made travel and communication between groups of native
peoples difficult. As a result, sub-Saharan cultures developed
independent of one another, with unique customs, beliefs, laws,
myths, and languages. There are more than a thousand
languages and dialects spoken in Africa!

How were African myths passed on?

Africans did not record their values, beliefs, or myths in writing, but they did express these things through diverse works of art. In many African cultures, masks, cave paintings, and ivory, stone, or wood sculptures were meaningful parts of individual and group religious worship.

Sub-Saharan societies generally were without written language until the 1800s. But many recorded vital knowledge by entrusting it to a member or members of their tribe. These "memory keepers" often memorized not only a society's history, heritage, customs, and myths, but also centuries' worth of family history for everyone in a village. In West Africa, these important caretakers of tradition are called *griots*. Part of a griot's role as an oral historian is to be a learned storyteller and entertainer. At ceremonies, griots play music, dance, and sing or chant. Griots and their traditions are still alive today.

What should you call Africa's supreme god?

Nearly all African peoples, including those who have not converted to the monotheistic religions of Islam or Christianity, believe in a supreme creator of all things. Because of Africa's many languages, this god has hundreds of names. In West Africa, the Yoruba call the god Olorun; the Dogon know it as Amma; to the Fon it is Mawa. The supreme being is generally a kind, all-powerful, all-knowing spirit who lives in heaven and gives life to and cares for all things. The being sometimes has a human form, with a face, body, and family; at other times it is an abstract, formless force. The lesser gods (such as those of water, the forest, or storms) and the spirits of real or mythical ancestors are considered to be more accessible to humans. So it is to these gods and spirits that temples are devoted and offerings made.

What do you get when you mix sand, a pigeon, and a hen?

The Yoruba peoples of West Africa say that in the beginning, there was only sky and a watery, marshy chaos that was neither sea nor land. The Supreme God, Olorun, lived in the sky, where the other gods attended him. One day Olorun called Orisha Nla, the Great God, into his presence and directed him to create land out of the chaos. To complete his task, Orisha Nla was given a pigeon, a five-toed hen, and a snail shell filled with sand. Orisha Nla descended to the marsh and poured the sand into the chaos. Then he set the pigeon and hen onto the sand and let them scratch, scratch, scratch until land was formed.

The Great God returned to Olorun to give him a progress report. The Supreme God dispatched a chameleon to inspect the land. When the chameleon came back with good things to say, Orisha Nla was allowed to finish his work. The first place of creation was called Ifé, meaning "wide" in the Yoruba language. Later the word *Ilé*, meaning "house," was added. Today the Yoruba consider Ilé-Ifé, in southwest Nigeria, their most sacred city.

What happened after Orisha Nla formed humans?

The work of creating the earth took four days. On the fifth day, Orisha Nla rested. Next Olorun sent Orisha Nla to plant trees that would provide wealth and nourishment to living things. Orisha Nla planted four kinds of trees, including the palm oil tree, whose nuts give oil and juice provides drink. When the Great God was done planting, the Supreme God made it rain, and the seedlings flourished into a great forest.

But whom would the forest sustain? Orisha Nla fashioned the first humans from earth. Only Olorun could give the people life, however. Orisha Nla, envious and curious to know how this was done, hid among the human forms one day after work. He waited for Olorun to come and breathe life into people, but the Supreme God knows all. Olorun would not do his work with Orisha Nla watching. Olorun put Orisha Nla into a deep sleep. When the Great God awoke, the humans were alive.

Today Olorun remains the only one who knows the secret of bestowing life. Orisha Nla still makes the forms of humans—sometimes leaving certain marks or deformities on them to show his annoyance—but only Olorun can bring them to life.

Why might African mythology have you seeing double?

Twins are a common theme in sub-Saharan mythology, especially among peoples of West Africa. The Dogon believe the universe was the work of the supreme god Amma. After throwing pellets of clay into space to create the stars, Amma molded the sun and moon out of pottery bowls that he surrounded with copper spirals. Next Amma threw a larger piece of clay into space to create the earth, with whom he mated to produce a set of divine twins; these were the forces of life in the world—water and light. Amma created four more pairs of creator twins, who organized earth and sky, day and night, the seasons, and human society.

The Fon believe that the universe was created and run by several pairs of twins. The Fons' supreme god, Mawa (a female, the moon, and controller of night), sometimes has a partner

twin named Lisa (a male, the sun, and spirit of day). Mawa and Lisa came together during a solar eclipse and became the parents of the other gods, seven pairs of twins. Mawa-Lisa assigned each pair a domain—earth, storms, iron, water, and forests; the two other pairs were sent to the sky to watch over humans.

Mawa and Lisa are among the few gods concerned with the sun and moon in sunny, tropical Africa. More common throughout Africa are spirits associated with water—a scarce resource. Gods of iron and blacksmithing were important, too. Often descendants of the supreme being, these gods had to make the earth habitable for humans by giving them tools for cultivating food and building shelters.

Why does a giant python encircle the earth?

Cosmic serpents are forces of creation in many African myths. In the Fon myth, Mawa's first creation was the serpent Dan Ayido Hwedo, whom she enlisted to help her make the world. When the earth was created but still unformed, the great  serpent wrapped his coils around the pieces of land and held them together to give humans a place to live. Dan Ayido Hwedo has a similar job today, holding his tail tightly in his mouth to sustain the earth. The serpent is constantly spiraling his coils around the earth, an action that sets the heavenly bodies— moon, stars, planets—in motion. Another version of the myth says that Dan Ayido Hwedo was made before Mawa, and that he carried the creator god in his mouth as the two formed the world. When they were done, Mawa was worried that the earth would sink under the weight of all the mountains, trees, and large animals. She asked Dan Ayido Hwedo to support the earth by coiling himself around the land.

MYTHIC LINKS In mythologies around the world, serpents with their tails in their mouths, forming a circle, are associated with eternity. The symbol is a common one in African art, appearing in paintings, fabrics, and wood and metal carvings.

What causes thunder and lightning?

Shango was known as an early king of the Yoruba peoples. Notorious for his strength but also his tyranny, Shango was said to breathe fire from his mouth. When the great warrior king was challenged by two of his ministers, he fled into the forest and hanged himself from a tree. From there he ascended to heaven, where he ruled as the god of thunder and lightning. Both these forces burst forth when Shango throws thunderbolts, or "thunder axes," down to earth.

Shango is usually depicted wearing a double-bladed ax on his head. Priests of the Yoruba often use symbolic thunder axes—canes with images of Shango and his headdress carved into the end—during religious rituals. The "axes" are thought to ward off the damage violent storms can cause.

Why is it dark at night?

According to the Kono people of Sierra Leone, in West Africa, when the world was new, it never really got dark. When the sun set, the moon cast enough light on the world to make everything clearly visible. All was fine and good until the supreme being asked Bat to carry a basket to the Moon. The basket had darkness inside. Bat did not know what the Moon was supposed to do with the darkness, but nevertheless he flew off on his mission. On his way to the Moon, however, Bat became tired and hungry. He set the basket down and went in search of food. While he was away, some other hungry animals came upon the basket and began pawing into it, looking for something to eat. Just as Bat returned, the animals pushed the cover off the basket and released darkness into the night. Ever since, Bat has slept during the day and spent the nights flying about, trying to catch the darkness and return it to the basket so he can take it to the Moon, as promised.

How did Mantis steal fire?

The praying mantis is the most important mythological creature of the San of southwest Africa. Some say Mantis invented words. He is also praised for obtaining fire. Mantis discovered fire when he smelled a delicious aroma wafting through the air. Following the scent, he peeked through some bushes to find Ostrich roasting his food over a fire. Mantis immediately wanted this wonderful source of heat for himself. He watched Ostrich finish his

meal and tuck the fire under his wing. As Ostrich left, Mantis came up behind him and told him about a fabulous fruit-bearing tree he had found. "Follow me!" Mantis said. "I will show you where it is." When they arrived, Mantis assured Ostrich that the best fruit was at the top. When Ostrich reached the high branches, he spread his wings wide to balance himself. Mantis grabbed the fire and ran. Ever since Ostrich has kept his wings close to his sides and has never attempted to fly.

How did Eshu use a two-colored hat to break up a lifelong friendship?

The Yoruba trickster Eshu (called Legba in other parts of West Africa) had knowledge of all languages and served as messenger between humans and the gods. His mischievous ways made him especially good at causing arguments between humans or between humans and gods. One day Eshu put on a hat that was black on one side, white on the other. He put his pipe in his mouth and hung his club over his shoulder so it extended behind him the same way his pipe did in front. Then Eshu walked the path between two farms that were worked by men who were best friends.

After Eshu had passed, the friends argued about the direction the stranger had been traveling and the color of his hat. The quarrel grew so heated that the king summoned the friends. Each man told the king the other was lying. Eshu arrived shortly and told the king that neither man was lying, but both were fools. When Eshu revealed what he had done, the king was furious. He sent his men after the god, but Eshu outran them all. The trickster set fire to many houses as he fled, offering to protect the possessions of those who were fleeing their houses. Instead, Eshu gave the belongings of the fire victims to others, spreading them in every direction.

How did Elephant and Hippo get into a tug-of-war?

In a story known through much of Africa, the trickster Hare decided to get married. He knew he had to clear his field for planting, to grow millet and support his wife, but he was much too lazy to do the work.

Lucky for Hare, he was as clever as he was lazy. He took a long rope down to the river and challenged Hippo to a game of tug-of-war, which Hippo declared he would win handily. Hare tied the rope around Hippo's body and said, "When you feel a tug on the rope, pull with all your might!" In the same way, Hare took the other end of the rope into the jungle and challenged Elephant. With a giant animal on either end of the rope, Hare went to the middle and began tugging in both directions. Soon Elephant and Hippo were pulling and struggling like mad, each wondering how a hare could put up such a fight. The contest lasted all day, and by sundown the tug-of-war had cleared all the bushes and churned up the ground—leaving the field ready for planting.

Trickster tales are popular throughout sub-Saharan Africa. Some of them were brought to the Americas by West Africans sold into slavery. Many stories about Hare fused with those of Rabbit, a Native American trickster of the Southeast United States (see page 125), and produced the character Brer Rabbit, a trickster in American folklore.

How did death come into the world?

Many African peoples believe that originally there was no death; earthly beings became mortal only after humans or animals misbehaved, broke a rule, or were lazy or ungrateful. According to the Nuer people of Sudan in eastern Africa, there was once a rope that connected heaven and earth. Any elderly person could climb the rope to heaven and have his or her youth restored by the High God. One day a hyena and a weaverbird climbed the rope. When they entered heaven, the High God instructed his attendants to watch these visitors carefully and not let them return to earth, where they were sure to cause trouble. The crafty animals escaped one night, however, and climbed down the rope. When the two had nearly reached the earth, the hyena cut the rope. The end that dangled from above was pulled up into heaven. Since people can no longer have their youth restored by the High God, they must now grow old and die.

What is the upside-down world?

Throughout Africa, belief in a world of the dead, where those who have died continue to exist as spirits, is common. Some peoples believe that departed spirits reside in the sky, while others say that they dwell underground. In both cases the world of the dead resembles the world of the living. The Kongo people of Zaire believe in an underworld that is nearly identical to the world of the living, with villages, hills, and water. The difference is that the underworld faces downward.

CHAPTER 7

NORTHERN EUROPE

IRELAND
AND SCANDINAVIA

The Norwegian god Odin on the door of
a Library of Congress building

CELTS

Were the Celts one big, happy family?

Though the Celts (pronounced "Kelts") dominated a vast part of
Europe between about 600 B.C.E. and C.E. 100, they were a
loosely connected band of tribes that never formed a single
nation. In fact, they only barely shared a common culture; each
tribe had its own territory and ruler and told its own myths.
Their languages, though different, all stemmed from Celtic,
which is why we call them Celts today. (They would not have
called themselves Celts.)

The Celts were less sophisticated than the early Greeks and
Romans in their architecture, scientific knowledge, military
strategy, and writing systems. However, they were successful

farmers, skilled horsemen, and talented metalworkers. The Celts were also proud warriors who fought with peoples they met when they moved into new territory. Sometimes they even fought among themselves to resolve tribal matters. Many Celtic myths glorified heroes as a way of setting examples of how human warriors should act in battle.

How much of Celtic mythology survives today?

Most Celtic myths of mainland Europe were lost when Romans took over the Celtic world, between 100 B.C.E. and C.E. 100. Ireland and a few remote areas of Great Britain (England, Scotland, and Wales) escaped Roman occupation, and the Celtic myths that survive are from these areas. The myths included in this book come from Ireland.

By the fifth century, the Romans had brought Christianity to Britain, and Saint Patrick had introduced the religion to Ireland. Even areas that had not been Romanized adopted Christianity. When Celtic myths were written down beginning between the sixth and eighth centuries, they were recorded by Christian monks. (Though the Celtic tradition of oral storytelling was strong, they had no written language of their own.) It is difficult to know how accurate and complete these retellings are because by this time, the stories were no longer purely Celtic. Celtic beliefs and rituals had become blurred by Christian ones, and many Celtic gods were "demoted" to the status of kings or heroes to be in line with the Christian belief in only one god. The two main manuscript collections that survive today are the *Lebor Gebala* from Ireland and the *Mabinogion* from Wales.

If you were a Celtic druid, you were a:

a) musician   b) poet   c) teacher

d) priest   e) all of the above

The answer is *e*. Celts had religious leaders called *druids*. These important members of Celtic society acted as priests, teachers, and advisors. Part of a druid's role was to pass on information

about laws, history, heroes, religion, and news events. The first step toward becoming a druid was to become a *bard*, or a learned musician and storyteller who memorized hundreds of legends and songs. It took many years of training to become a bard, and up to twenty years to gain the knowledge necessary to become a druid.

Were the Celts the first peoples to live in Ireland?

Irish Celtic mythology tells of a series of five mythical peoples who invaded Ireland before the Celts arrived. The last group, gods called the Tuatha Dé Danann, defeated the previous group of invaders, former slaves called the Firbolg, in the First Battle of Magh Tuiredh. The victorious Tuatha Dé Danann drove the Firbolg from the island.

Then the Tuatha Dé Danann's rule was challenged by the Formorians, a race of violent sea gods with only one arm and one leg each, who rose from the waters around Ireland. The Formorians' leader was Balor, a Cyclops whose dangerous gaze killed anyone he looked upon. Four servants were required to lift Balor's one eyelid, which they did at the Second Battle of Magh Tuiredh. When the Tuatha Dé Danann leader, Lugh, saw Balor's eyelid being raised, he fired a rock from his slingshot straight into Balor's eye. The blow pushed the awful eyeball back into Balor's head, turning the deadly gaze on his own Formorians. The Formorians who escaped the gaze scattered, leaving the Tuatha Dé Danann triumphant.

Who defeated the Tuatha Dé Danann?

The Tuatha Dé Danann did not have long to savor their hard-won victory over the Formorians. Soon a ship landed on their shores. Assuming it was an invasion, the Tuatha Dé Danann killed the ship's captain. The captain was Ith, a Spaniard who lived in a great tower. He had spied Ireland from his windows and was merely curious about the island. When Ith's body was returned to his kinsmen in Spain, a true invasion force was mustered. At the head of this force was Milesius (also called Mil), Ith's father. Milesius did not survive the voyage to Ireland, but his remaining sons did. They landed and waged a vengeful battle against the Tuatha Dé Danann. In the end, Milesius's sons were victorious. One of the leaders split the island of Ireland in two, giving the half that is underground to the Tuatha Dé Danann, who became fairies. The sons of Milesius stayed aboveground and became the first Celts.

WORLD OF WORDS

The word *banshee* comes from the Celtic *bean sidhe*, which means "woman of the fairies." These Tuatha Dé Danann women were said to live beneath Ireland's grassy hillsides. The eerie wail of a banshee was thought to mean that a human death would soon occur.

Why did Finn MacCool suck his thumb?

Finn MacCool was the great-grandson of Nuada of the Silver Hand, chief of the Tuatha Dé Danann. His father was a warrior who had died in battle, so for instruction in life the fatherless child sought the druid Finegas. Finegas lived near the River Boyne, where he had been trying for seven years to catch the Salmon of Knowledge. Whoever ate this fish would enjoy boundless wisdom.

Soon after Finn's arrival, Finegas caught the prized fish. He gave it to his pupil to cook, with strict instructions not to eat any of it. When Finn brought the cooked fish to Finegas, the druid asked Finn if he had done as he was told. Finn said he had, though he had burned his thumb on the salmon while turning it on the spit. To ease the pain, Finn said, he stuck his thumb in his mouth. Finegas knew then that Finn was meant to have the salmon. From that time on, Finn only had to put his thumb in his mouth and the answer to any question would come to him. Finn MacCool grew up to be the greatest leader of the Fianna, a famous band of warriors who swore to protect the king of Ireland.

Who was Ireland's greatest Celtic hero?

Cuchulainn was the son of Lugh, the Irish Celtic sun god. Known for his strength and bravery—but also for his temper—Cuchulainn transformed into a frightful being in battle. His body began to tremble wildly, and his heels and calves appeared in the front of his legs. One of his eyes disappeared inside his head while the other bulged out, huge and red, from his cheek. His jaw grew until a man's head could fit inside it. After fighting, three vats of cold water were needed to cool Cuchulainn's battle frenzy and restore him to his normal self.

 Women such as Scathach appear as warriors and war goddesses in Celtic mythology because the Celts had a strong tradition of women as warriors and leaders. In C.E. 697 a group of Christian leaders banned females from battle, but some continued to take up arms long after that.

Cuchulainn was trained in the arts of war by Scathach, a warrior princess in the Land of Shadows. The hero drilled long and hard with Scathach, for he was intent on winning the hand of a woman named Emer. (Emer's father, Forgall, wanted Cuchulainn to establish himself as a true warrior before he would give up his daughter.) After a year and a day of training with Scathach, Cuchulainn called at Fogall's castle to claim his bride. Forgall still was not satisfied, and a battle ensued. Cuchulainn drove

Forgall to the castle walls, where he jumped to his death to escape the hero.

How did Cuchulainn lose his son?

Cuchulainn took Emer as his wife. He did not know, however, that he had a son from a previous relationship with Aoifa, the sister of Scathach. When Cuchulainn left Aoifa, he had given her a gold ring.

Fifteen years later, a teenage boy named Conlai appeared in Ulster, where Cuchulainn lived. Conlai was a skilled fighter, and in a battle with the Ulster men he killed Conall, Cuchulainn's foster brother. Cuchulainn, thus provoked, drew his sword on the boy. As the two engaged in combat, Cuchulainn was impressed with the boy's sword-wielding skill. But soon his temper got the best of him and Cuchulainn thrust his sword into Conlai's heart, spying only too late Aoife's gold ring on the boy's finger. Overcome with sadness and guilt, Cuchulainn carried his dying son to his house and buried him there.

What did Queen Maeve want from Ulster?

Queen Maeve, also called Queen Medb, was the warrior queen of Connacht, a kingdom in Ireland. Maeve's husband, King Ailill, had a splendid White-Horned Bull. This made Maeve desire the enormous Brown Bull of Ulster for herself.

Maeve summoned her troops and commanded them to invade Ulster. The queen knew that Ulster's warrior Cuchulainn was nearly unbeatable in combat, but she sent her army to invade at a time when all the other heroes in Ulster were under a curse of the war goddess Macha. Cuchulainn alone was strong enough to fight despite the curse. For five days he used strength and skill to slaughter Queen Maeve's invaders single-handedly, slowing their advance until the curse wore off the other Ulstermen. Despite his valiant efforts, Cuchulainn suffered a terrible stomach wound. Knowing his time was nearly up, Cuchulainn tied himself to a tree so he would die on his feet. Ulster mourned the loss of their great hero.

NORSE

Who were the Vikings?

The Norse were a European people who spread from present-day Germany and Poland into England and Scandinavia (Sweden, Norway, and Denmark) in the fourth and fifth centuries. From about 700 to 1000, the Norse were also known as Vikings. Many Vikings left their homes in Scandinavia and raided, traded, and colonized their way through parts of western Europe, Russia, and North America. The Vikings were expert shipbuilders and able navigators who traveled farther than any other Europeans of the time. They founded Russia and became the first-known peoples to sail to Iceland, Greenland, and Canada.

The Vikings had a reputation for being thuggish brutes. Indeed, their imposing ships and sudden, violent raids terrified many a local population. But though they did plunder treasure and capture slaves, for the most part Vikings were seeking new trading markets and farmlands, not peoples to conquer. When they weren't raiding villages, fiercely competitive Viking men challenged one another in sports, games, and contests. Courage and strength were the standards by which Norsemen measured their worth. Accordingly, Viking myths are rich in heroes and heroines, battles, and violence.

Did the Vikings have a written language?

The Vikings had an alphabet of letters called *runes*, which were believed to be magical symbols with power to cast spells both good and evil. But few Norsemen learned to read or write the runic language. Instead, Viking histories and stories, or sagas, were memorized and passed down by word of mouth. After a feast, a poet or a more sophisticated orator, called a *skald*, would entertain people with stories. For his wisdom, a skald was considered as powerful as a warrior.

The Viking myths that survive today were recorded in two main works of Icelandic literature, the *Poetic Edda* (also called the *Elder Edda*) and the *Prose Edda*. The eddas date from the 1200s. By this time, Vikings had adopted Christianity and mostly given up the gods and stories of their old religion. The *Poetic Edda* was probably written by several different poets. The *Prose Edda* was written by an Icelandic chieftain and scholar named Snorri Sturluson (c. 1179–1241), who recorded all he could learn of the ancient myths before they were completely lost.

Who were the first Norse gods?

Before the world existed, there was a huge, yawning emptiness called Ginnungagap. To the north was the frozen realm of Niflheim, and to the south lay the fiery region of Muspell. Over time sparks from Muspell leaped and mingled with ice from Niflheim. Icicles melted and dripped into Ginnungagap, where they eventually formed two gigantic creatures.

The first creature was the evil Ymir; the second was a cow named Audhumla. Ymir grew tall and strong drinking Audhumla's milk. One night while Ymir slept, three frost giants grew from his body. Audhumla, too, found life. While she fed herself by licking the salty ice of Niflheim with her rough tongue, she uncovered a creature named Buri. Buri had a son named Bor, who in turn had sons named Odin, Vili, and Ve. These were the first gods. Odin, Vili, and Ve were full of honor and virtue, and they quickly tired of Ymir's tyranny. Led by Odin, the gods overtook the evil giant and killed him.

Where did the first people live?

The three gods used Ymir's body to create the earth and sky. The sky was held up at each corner—north, south, east, and west—by four dwarves, which the gods created from maggots that were eating Ymir's body. Other dwarves were sent to live and mine ore belowground where, despite their ill natures, they made glorious weapons and treasures for the gods. To light the world, the gods gathered sparks from Muspell and scattered them in the sky. Then Odin and his brothers created a girl named Sun and a boy named Moon, and set them in their paths across the sky.

The first humans were created when Odin, Vili, and Ve came upon two trees—an ash and elm—on the seashore. From the ash the gods created a man named Ask, and from the elm they made a woman named Embla. Each god endowed the humans with special gifts, including breath, movement, understanding, speech, hearing, and sight. Then they placed the people in Midgard, the world they had created from Ymir's body.

MYTHIC VOICES:

66 From Ymir's flesh
the earth was made
and from his blood the seas,
crags from his bones,
trees from his hair,
and from his skull the sky.

From his eyebrows

the blessed gods

made Midgard for the sons of man,

and from his brains

were created

all storm-threatening clouds."

—FROM *THE PROSE EDDA OF SNORRI STURLUSON*, TRANSLATED BY JEAN I. YOUNG

Norse mythology has nine different worlds, each of them home to a certain race of beings. All of the worlds were entwined in the roots and branches of the great World Tree, Yggdrasill. Various routes linked the realms of Yggdrasill and allowed steady, if perilous, traffic among worlds. The most celebrated path was Bifrost, the rainbow bridge between Asgard and Midgard, heaven and earth. Messages traveled between the worlds too. A squirrel constantly scurried up and down the tree, carrying insults between the destructive serpent Nidhogg, who gnawed at the tree roots in Niflheim, and an eagle perched on the highest treetop who kept watch over the worlds of Yggdrasill.

Who were the Norse gods' archenemies?

After Ymir's death, the three surviving giants sailed to a faraway land, Jotunheim, and started a new race of frost giants. These giants never forgave the gods for what Odin and his brothers had done to Ymir. Forevermore the gods and giants were at odds.

The Norse equated frost giants with Scandinavia's menacing, ice-capped mountains. When frigid air blew down from the peaks, it was said to be the giants' breath nipping springtime buds. When an avalanche tumbled from a lofty height, it was thought that a giant was shaking ice and snow from its shoulders or brow.

Who helped Odin defend the world?

Odin felt a special responsibility to protect the world from doom. He and his wife, Frigga, the goddess of knowledge, had several sons—all of whom helped ward off destruction. Their eldest son, Thor, was the strongest of all the gods and second only to Odin in greatness. As the god of thunder, Thor used his magic hammer to produce thunder and lightning and to protect gods and humans from the frost giants. Another son was Tyr, a god of war and the bravest of all Norse deities.

⊙ MYTHIC LINKS If the impressive powers of thunder and lightning have ever left you awestruck or quaking with fear, imagine how the ancients—without our modern, sturdy houses—must have felt. It's no wonder thunder gods feature prominently in many cultures' mythologies. Thor has parallels in the thunder-wielding gods Zeus (of the Greeks), Indra (of India), and Shango (of the Yoruba in Africa).

Who was Asgard's mysterious visitor?

Odin and his brothers built magnificent halls of gold and silver for the gods and goddesses in Asgard. Soon after that, a mysterious stranger arrived with a horse in tow and offered to build a wall around Asgard, to protect it from the frost giants and other enemies. The gods wanted to fortify their realm. But they were outraged when the stranger told them that in return, he wanted the sun, the moon, and Freja, the beautiful goddess of love. The gods only agreed to this deal on one condition— one they were sure the stranger couldn't meet. The trickster god Loki suggested that the stranger must complete the wall within six months. The stranger agreed and set to work with his stallion.

Month after month the wall grew higher. With it mounted the gods' fear that the stranger would fulfill his end of the deal. It had become clear that the stallion was doing most of the work, hauling heavy stones day and night. The gods clamored for Loki to stop the stranger from finishing the wall before they lost their dear Freja and the world's light. Loki, known for his craftiness and shape-shifting, turned himself into a graceful mare and lured the stranger's powerful stallion into the woods. The stranger ran after the horses but could not catch them, no matter how fast he ran.

When the stranger realized the wall would not be finished on time, he flew into a rage. His anger exposed his identity: The stranger was a frost giant! Thor used his mighty hammer to knock the giant dead, safeguarding the sun, moon, and Freja.

Why did Loki visit the dwarves?

Thor's wife, Sif, had exceptionally beautiful hair made of pure gold. Late one night Loki—who was sometimes mischievous—crept into Sif's bedroom and cut it off. When Thor saw his wife, he went after the trickster, threatening to take Loki's life if he did not make up for his cruel act. "I will restore Sif's hair—I promise!" Loki cried. Then he sped to the dwarves and asked them to spin new golden locks for the goddess.

The dwarves did as Loki asked. Eager to show their skill as masters of their trade, the dwarves created other marvelous treasures for the gods. For the god Frey, who ruled rain and sunlight, they fashioned a ship that could be folded up and carried in a pocket. For Odin they made a spear that always hit its target.

WORLD OF WORDS

You may not realize it, but you talk about Norse gods all the time. In the English language, the names of four days of the week come from Norse gods:

Tuesday	Tyr's-day
Wednesday	Woden's-day (Odin was also known as Woden)
Thursday	Thor's-day
Friday	Frigga's-day

Delighted, Loki took the gifts and headed for Asgard. But then he had an idea: He stopped at another workshop and challenged the dwarves there, Sindri and Brok, to make gifts for the gods as splendid as the ones he was carrying. "I'll wager my head that you can't create anything so stunning," Loki said. "Only you must not hurt any other part of my body." The dwarves set to work.

Did Loki lose his head to Sindri and Brok?

Afraid that Sindri and Brok would win the bet, Loki transformed into a fly and repeatedly bit one of the dwarves to distract him from his work. But the dwarves would not be deterred. They created a magic bull that could run over land and water. Then they made a giant gold ring called Draupnir. Last they fashioned an enormous hammer, called Mjollnir, that always smashed its target and returned to the thrower's hand like a boomerang.

The dwarves traveled to Asgard with Loki and presented their gifts. The gods and goddesses were astounded by the beauty of the new treasures. Frey received the boat and the magic bull, Odin the golden ring and the spear, and Thor the mighty hammer. The gods declared that the hammer was the most exquisite work, and Sindri and Brok demanded their payment— Loki's head.

As Brok approached with a knife, Loki reminded the dwarf that he had promised them his head, but that did not include any part of his neck. When Brok realized he could not cut off the trickster's head, he lowered his sword. Though Loki had worked his usual mischief, the gods were pleased to have their new treasures.

 Some Vikings wore charms shaped like Thor's hammer for good luck and protection from evil. Even after the Norse converted to Christianity, many solicited help from Thor when they were in the heat of battle.

Why did Thor and Loki dress up as women to visit Jotunheim?

One morning Thor awoke to find his mighty hammer missing. Immediately he called for Loki and accused him of stealing it. Loki professed his innocence. To prove it, he turned himself into a falcon and searched the nine worlds for the hammer. He found it in Jotunheim with Thrym, the king of the frost giants. When Loki demanded the hammer, the giant refused. Thrym said he would only return the hammer when the goddess Freja was his bride.

Loki flew back to Asgard with this news, and Freja cried out in protest. The god Heimdall had an idea. "You yourself must go to Thrym, dressed as a bride," he told Thor. Now it was Thor's turn to protest. "I will not be humiliated by dressing as a woman!" Thor cried. But Odin reminded his son that the magic hammer, in the hands of the giants, could do great harm to Asgard. Thor relented and put on a bridal dress, veil, and Freja's jewelry. Loki dressed as a woman too, disguised as Thor's maidservant.

When they arrived at Thrym's hall after eight days of travel, they were met with great cheering and celebration. At the wedding feast, Thrym was amazed to see his bride eat so well— eight salmon and an entire ox—and drink three barrels of beer. "My mistress has been so excited about her marriage that she has not eaten in eight days," Loki explained in a high voice.

When Thrym zeroed in to steal a kiss from his bride, he was stunned by the blazing eyes he saw through the veil. "My mistress has been so eager for you that she has not slept in eight days," Loki squeaked. Just before the marriage ceremony, Thrym brought the mighty hammer into the hall to exchange it for his bride. Thrym laid the hammer in Thor's lap as a blessing, and Thor immediately set to wielding blow after blow until all the giants were dead. Thor and Loki returned to Asgard in triumph.

 The spell of Andvari's ring might make you think of J. R. R. Tolkien's *Lord of the Rings* stories. Tolkien was influenced by Norse mythology, and also by Greek and Roman mythology and the legends of King Arthur. Tolkien saw his mythology of Middle-Earth as the mythology of what might have come before, and given common ground to, these other mythic traditions.

What did the dragon Fafnir guard?

Loki, Odin, and the god Honir were wandering through Midgard when Loki accidentally killed the son of the farmer Hreidmar. When the gods arrived at Hreidmar's farmhouse to request a night's lodging, Hreidmar summoned his two surviving sons, Fafnir and Regin. Then he declared his plan: He would hold Odin and Honir hostage until Loki could deliver, as ransom for his son, a vast quantity of gold. Loki was sent to capture the enormous treasure of the dwarf Andvari.

Loki ventured to the underground lake where Andvari lived. After capturing the dwarf in a magic net, Loki issued threat after threat until Andvari finally surrendered his immense horde of gold, including a magic gold-making ring. But as Loki departed with the treasure, bitter Andvari laid a curse on the ring: Whoever possessed it would be doomed.

Indeed, Hreidmar held the treasure only a short while. For Fafnir had come under the ring's spell, and with the help of his brother Regin, he killed his father and seized the treasure. Fafnir became so consumed with greed and evil that he turned into a dragon and withdrew to a forest lair to guard the cursed treasure.

How did the Norse hero Sigurd slay Fafnir?

Myths of heroes who slay dragons have been popular in Northern European mythology for more than a thousand years. Perhaps the best loved of these stories involves Sigurd, the greatest hero of Norse mythology.

Many aspiring heroes were drawn to Fafnir's lair in search of fame and fortune. None returned but Sigurd. Urged and aided by Regin, Sigurd approached the dragon's lair and found the path the monster used when traveling to the river for water. Armed with his father's sword, a gift from Odin, Sigurd lay in Fafnir's path and slew the dragon from beneath as the beast passed by.

When the dragon was dead, Regin asked Sigurd to cut out its heart so he could eat it. But while Sigurd was roasting the heart over a fire that evening, he touched the meat with his fingers and then licked off the blood. Suddenly Sigurd could understand the birds singing in the trees. He overheard them say that the dragon's heart was magical, and also that Regin was plotting to kill him and seize Fafnir's treasure. Sigurd promptly cut off Regin's head and ate the dragon's heart himself. Thereafter Sigurd was the wisest of men.

MYTHIC LINKS The similarity between Sigurd gaining wisdom from the blood of the dragon's heart and the Celtic myth of Finn MacCool and the Salmon of Knowledge is an example of how the Norse were influenced by the Celts. Vikings often raided Ireland; sometimes they even set up camps, from which they launched raids on other parts of Ireland and Britain.

How did a sprig of mistletoe kill Balder?

Balder was the fairest of all the gods and the clear favorite of his parents, Odin and Frigga. When Balder began having dreams of his own destruction, Frigga tried to protect her son. She traveled around the world demanding vows from every thing, whether living or nonliving, that they would never harm Balder. Thereafter, the gods made sport of hurling all manner of spears and stones at Balder, knowing he could not be hurt. This was meant to honor Balder, and all the gods cheered his invincibility . . . all the gods but one.

Loki was jealous of Balder, and he used his cunning to learn that there was one plant that had not given its oath to Frigga. This was the mistletoe, which Frigga thought too young and feeble to do any harm. On its own, it probably wouldn't have. But Loki made a dart of a mistletoe branch and gave it to the blind god Hoder, the twin of Balder. Loki helped the unsuspecting Hoder throw and guide the dart straight at Balder's heart, killing the fair god instantly.

Devastated, Frigga begged someone to visit Hel, Loki's gruesome daughter and goddess of the underworld, and attempt to bring Balder back. The god Hermod, another of Balder's brothers, courageously volunteered. When he pleaded with Hel to let Balder return to Asgard, Hel replied that she would allow it only on one condition: if all the beings and things in the world wept for Balder. If even one refused, Balder would remain in the underworld.

Hermod sped back to Asgard, and gods proceeded to spread Hel's message far and wide. Every thing, from stones to trees to humans, showed their love for the Good God by weeping. But there was one lone giantess living in a cave who refused to shed a tear. The giantess said that Balder had been nothing to her, so she had no feelings one way or the other. She was Loki in disguise. Hel heard her words and refused to release Balder from the world of the dead.

Was Loki punished for his hand in Balder's death?

Loki knew that his actions would bring the wrath of the gods upon him, for he had changed from being a mischievous prankster to being a twisted figure. Loki fled. With the gods on his tail, he transformed into a salmon and hid in a creek. Yet the angry gods fished him out and took him to a dark cave. There they tied him to three rocks. Above his head they fixed a serpent that dripped poisonous venom onto his face. This was how Loki was forced to await the end of the world. Though Loki's wife, Sigun, sat by his side and held a cup beneath the snake to keep the venom from hitting Loki's face, she could not stop it entirely. Whenever Sigun had to take the cup away to empty it, the venom fell on Loki and burned his skin. At these times, the Norse believed, the earth shook with Loki's pain.

How will the world end?

Ragnarok is the unavoidable time of destruction of the world, a battle between the gods and giants in which everything is consumed by flames and floods.

Ragnarok begins when Loki breaks from his bonds and leads the giants against the gods of Asgard. He is accompanied by his monstrous children: Hel, the ferocious wolf Fenrir, and the enormous Midgard Serpent. Together the enemies of the Aesir converge on Bifrost. Odin's son Heimdall, standing guard at the rainbow bridge, sounds a warning trumpet to signal the arrival of the terrible army.

On the vast Plain of Vigrid, the fighting begins. Odin leads the gods into battle but is eventually swallowed by Fenrir. Thor slays the Midgard Serpent but is poisoned by its venom and perishes. Fenrir devours the sun and moon. The stars fall from the sky, the mountains crumble, and the fire god, Surt, sets the world ablaze. The universe and everything in it is engulfed in flames. The ashes from the fire are consumed by the rising sea. Time is no more.

But Ragnarok is not the end. Before the sun is swallowed, she gives birth to a daughter, the sun of the next world. A pair of humans survive to repopulate the earth. A handful of children of the gods are reborn, and together they bring forth a new world of peace, order, and prosperity—a world better than the one before it.

Odin knew that Ragnarok was coming and that no amount of resistance could change its outcome. Yet he and the gods prepared to fight to the finish, for they believed as Norse warriors did: Despite impending death, a fighter could win honor by displaying bravery and courage up until the very moment he died. As Sigurd said to a demigoddess in the *Elder Edda*, "I will not flee though you foretell my death—I was never called a coward."

CHAPTER 8

THE AMERICAS

NORTH, MESO, AND SOUTH AMERICA

Navajo man preparing sand painting

 NORTH AMERICA

What do North American mythologies have in common?

The earliest Americans were small groups of hunter-gatherers who followed game—bison, woolly mammoths, and other animals—over a land bridge from Asia to present-day Alaska perhaps thirty or forty thousand years ago. (Today, sea levels are higher, and the land bridge is covered by the Bering Strait.) Over thousands of years, these peoples, commonly called Native Americans or American Indians, spread south and east through North America.

Some American Indians remained nomadic hunter-gatherers, while others settled in small farming communities. North America's varied climate, landscapes, and wildlife inspired equally varied lifestyles, beliefs, and mythologies. But some themes that are common across nearly all North American Indian cultures include belief in a Great Spirit who made the world, or at least inspired its creation, and belief that supernatural power exists in all living and natural things, from rodents to rain to rocks. (Accordingly, many myths demonstrate how to treat the living world with respect.) Animals are believed to have a soul just as humans do, and respect is paid to the spirit of an animal about to be hunted. Also nearly universal are tribal *shamans*, or medicine men who have powerful abilities to communicate with the spirit world.

Who told the myths?

When Europeans began exploring North America in the sixteenth century, North American Indians had no written records. Myths were not written down but passed on orally from older to younger generations. This important job was only entrusted to members of the community who were especially good storytellers or had specially trained memories.

Indians also held many myth-related dances and ceremonies, many of which are still performed today. For example, the Navajo of the Southwest make sand paintings that are believed to cure participants of illness. These paintings show scenes from Navajo myths and are created using colored powders made from charcoal, pollen, flowers, and cornmeal. When the painting is finished, the curing ceremony begins with the recitation of the creation myth. The hope is that in reenacting the creation, the patient will be "reborn"—or cured.

Where did humans come from?

In many North American Indian creation myths, the earth was said to have begun as a vast sea with no land exposed. According to the Iroquois of the Northeast, the Sky Chief, who lived above the watery world, sent a woman pregnant with humankind down to earth to start a new race of people. When the water animals below saw the Sky Woman falling toward them, they realized she would have nowhere to stand. The animals worked together, gathering mud from the bottom of the sea and piling it on the back of Turtle to create land for the woman. The birds supported the falling woman on their backs and lowered her safely when the new earth was finished.

In contrast to the Iroquois myth, many other American Indian myths describe how humans climbed or were led up to earth from underground. In the Southwest, the Pueblo peoples tell how the Great Spirit Awonawilona created Mother Earth and Father Sky. Deep within the earth, in the innermost of Mother Earth's four wombs, the beginnings of the first humans were formed. Mother Earth and Father Sky then created twins who placed the sun in the sky and built a ladder of vines and trees between Mother Earth's wombs. The twins instructed the developing creatures until they were ready to be led upward from womb to womb, eventually emerging on the earth's surface. Having always been underground, the first humans were scaly black creatures with short tails, owls' eyes, huge ears, and webbed feet. The great medicine man Yanauluha changed these beings into recognizable humans by teaching them how to farm, structure their communities, and survive on the earth.

Kivas in San Juan County, New Mexico

Pueblo *kivas* are circular underground temples used for prayer and fertility ceremonies. They were built belowground to be closer to Mother Earth's wombs, where humans had been formed.

Where did corn come from?

There were many myths about the origin of corn, American Indians' most important food crop. The myth of the Penobscot peoples of the Northeast describes how First Mother, the first woman on Earth, offered up her body in order to feed her starving people.

First Mother received her name after marrying an earth-dwelling spirit and having many children and grandchildren. The people multiplied such that the land grew crowded, and soon there was not enough game to feed everyone. The children begged First Mother for food. With tears in her eyes, she told them she had none. But she told them to be patient; she would fill their bellies. Then First Mother told her husband that he must kill her and drag her body over an empty patch of earth until all her flesh was gone. Then he was to bury her bones at the center of the patch, wait seven moons, and come back. At first her husband refused, but First Mother was firm about her wishes.

Seven moons later, First Mother's husband and children found the patch of land covered with tall green plants—corn. First Mother's flesh had yielded this nourishing crop. If the people always took good care of First Mother's sacrificed body, she would sustain them forever.

> **MYTHIC LINKS**   In many cultures' mythologies, the earth and its fertility were said to be controlled or embodied by female gods. New plant life arose out of the goddess's earth-body, just as new human life emerges from a human woman's body. First Mother and Mother Earth share similarities with the Greek goddess Gaia, whose body also became the earth.

How did Feather Woman turn the world upside down?

The Blackfoot of the Northwest tell a myth about the young maiden Feather Woman, who fell in love with the Morning Star and went to live with him and his parents, Sun and Moon, in the Sky Country.

Soon Feather Woman gave birth to a son, Poia. Morning Star gave his wife everything she wanted. But he told her the one thing she must not do was dig up the giant turnip that grew outside their lodge. Feather Woman initially obeyed this command, but eventually she grew so curious that she began to dig around the turnip. When two birds flew by, she asked for help pulling the giant turnip from the ground. The turnip loosed with a *pop!* and left a gaping hole in the ground. Feather Woman peeked through the hole into the world below— her world. She spied a Blackfoot village and grew terribly homesick. At the same time, she was full of guilt and remorse for disobeying Morning Star.

That evening Morning Star returned to the lodge very sad. He told Feather Woman that she must be banished from the Sky Country for what she had done. Morning Star also told his wife that she had inflicted unhappiness and death on her people by her disobedience. Devastated, Feather Woman returned to earth with Poia. So great was her grief that she died within days.

⊚ **MYTHIC LINKS** Like Feather Woman, the Greeks' Pandora also unleashed grief and suffering on her people, in her case by lifting the lid of the jar she was told never to open. Another comparable figure is Eve in the Bible, who first ate the forbidden fruit in the Garden of Eden and thus was expelled from paradise with her husband, Adam. Thereafter humankind faced sickness, pain, toil, and death.

The mighty warrior Glooskap was defeated by a baby.

True. Glooskap, a creator god and great hero of the Algonquin peoples, was ruler of man and beast. He wandered the world defeating evil in all forms, whether ghost, spirit, human, or animal. When he had been gone many months, he returned home to find his wife tending something he had never seen before. This thing was small and near the ground. It kept Glooskap's wife so busy that she hardly noticed her husband's arrival. Glooskap demanded to know what this tiny creature was. His wife replied that it was the mighty Wasis, master of all the world. "He is not master of me!" Glooskap cried. "I have defeated enemies far and wide. I will not be defeated in my own home!" Glooskap walked straight up to the Wasis and challenged him to a duel. The Wasis only gurgled. Glooskap yelled at the Wasis, proclaiming his supremacy. This time the Wasis screamed, and continued screaming. "Stop that!" Glooskap shouted. But the Wasis only wailed louder. Desperate, Glooskap danced and sang until finally the Wasis stopped crying. The Wasis chucked and murmured a happy "Goo" as Glooskap collapsed in exhaustion. So it was that the hero who had defeated all in his path found that the wailing Wasis—a baby—was the only power that could defeat him. Every time a baby wears a smile and says "Goo!" it is remembering its triumph over Glooskap.

What happened when Wolf and Coyote disagreed about death?

The Shoshoni of the western Plains told a myth about the two most important animals of ancient times, Coyote and Wolf. Coyote was a trickster figure who was often at odds with Wolf, and whose foolish, deceptive ways usually backfired.

In the beginning, Wolf said that death should be temporary: When a living thing died, he or she should only have to shoot an arrow into the earth beneath him to be brought back to life. Just to be difficult, Coyote refused, saying the world would get too crowded that way. Wolf gave in but secretly decided that Coyote's son would be the first to die. When Coyote found his son dead, he told Wolf that he had changed his mind. But this time Wolf refused, saying it was Coyote himself who had wanted death to be final. And that's the way it has been for all living things ever since.

 In life, as in myth, coyotes are cunning, swift, and impossible to tame. They can seem almost indestructible—a bit like the cartoon character Wile E. Coyote. The modern trickster from the *Roadrunner* cartoon was inspired by, and shares many qualities with, Coyote from American Indian mythology. Coyote appears in myths of the Southwest and Plains, but he is only one of many Indian tricksters who share similar characteristics and stories. Other North American tricksters include Rabbit, Spider, and Raven.

How did Deer get his antlers?

A Cherokee myth tells how Deer and the trickster Rabbit decided to have a contest to see which of them was the fastest. Being that both their heads were smooth as basketballs, the animals fashioned a grand pair of antlers as a prize for whoever won the race.

The contest was to take place in a dense thicket. Rabbit said he was not familiar with the area and asked if he could explore it before the race began. The animals agreed, and Rabbit disappeared. But when Rabbit did not return for quite some time, the animals went looking for him—and found him hacking and gnawing a path through the brush! Furious at Rabbit's attempt to cheat and deceive them, the animals awarded the beautiful antlers to Deer. And since Rabbit was so good at gnawing thickets, he was given the task of doing that forever. He still does it today, while Deer proudly displays his antlers.

MESOAMERICA

Who were the Maya?

By 7000 B.C.E., the peoples who had come across the land bridge from Asia to North America had spread through Central and South America as well. Many of these peoples remained hunters, gatherers, and fishermen and lived in small groups. But some, like the Maya of Mexico and Central America (an area sometimes called Mesoamerica), built a complex civilization beginning around C.E. 300. The Maya Empire remained at its height until about 900, though parts of the civilization lasted through the early 1500s.

The Maya Empire consisted of individual city-states, each with separate rulers. These rulers often fought each other and took captives, which were offered to the gods as human sacrifices. To the Maya, such offerings sustained the gods—who sustained the world—and brought fertility and prosperity to the people.

The Mayan pantheon of gods was quite complicated. Individual Mayan gods could take on several different names and forms, ranging from human to animal to plant to thunder. Gods could also be present in the sun, moon, planets, and stars. The Maya charted the heavens and became expert astronomers in order to forecast the gods' actions. They also studied advanced mathematics, used a complex calendar, and developed the Americas' only comprehensive writing system. The Maya used their writing system, one of hieroglyphs, to record the *Popol Vuh* ("Council Book"), an ancient, sacred text that tells the history of the Mayan people from their creation up through the arrival of Spanish conquerors in the 1540s.

Why were humans created, according to Mayan mythology? To:

a) serve the gods   b) replace the gods

c) play soccer, chess, and video games

The answer is letter *a*. In the beginning, all that existed beneath the sky was a watery world. Gucumatz, a feathered serpent, swam to the surface of the water with other water-dwelling gods and spoke to Heart of Heaven, a sky god, and his brethren. The gods talked about creating a place of mountains and land, trees and flowers, plants and animals. As they spoke, their words became reality. The world was born.

When the gods realized that none of their creations could worship them properly, they decided to fashion humans. First they tried making people from mud, but these creatures dissolved in water and could not stand upright. Next they tried molding people from tree branches. These wooden people kept their shape in water and could stand upright. But they were heartless and stiff and did not respect the gods, who sent demons to eat the wooden people and a flood to destroy them. It was back to the drawing board.

After much deliberation, the gods decided to try grinding a paste from white and yellow corn kernels and molding humans from the dough. Finally the gods were successful! The new people were wise and thoughtful and quickly gave thanks to the gods. In fact, the gods soon realized that these people were too perfect—too knowledgeable and too similar to themselves. To remedy this, the gods diminished the people's eyesight. This allowed humans to see only what was around them, and left the all-powerful wisdom of the heavens to the gods. Thus the Mayans' ancestors were born.

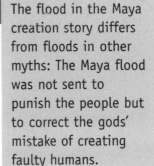

The flood in the Maya creation story differs from floods in other myths: The Maya flood was not sent to punish the people but to correct the gods' mistake of creating faulty humans.

MYTHIC VOICES:

66 We really give you thanks, two and three times! We have been created, we have been given a mouth and a face, we speak, we hear, we think, and walk; we

feel perfectly, and we know what is far and what is near. We also see the large and the small in the sky and on earth. We give you thanks, then, for having created us, oh, Creator and Maker!**

—From *Popol Vuh: The Sacred Book of the Ancient Quiche Maya*, English version by Delia Goetz and Sylvanus G. Morley, from the translation by Adrián Recinos

Did Mayans play basketball?

The Maya and other Mesoamerican cultures played a sport similar to basketball, in which the players' goal was to drive a rubber ball through rings attached to the court's walls, using only their hips and elbows. The game was not just for fun; it had religious and mythological importance. The court symbolized the world, and the ball represented the sun. Players had to keep the ball moving and aloft in order to fuel the sun's journey across the sky. The game was fast and dangerous. Despite protective pads and clothing, many players were injured. But that was nothing compared to what happened to the losing team: They were often sacrificed to the sun god, Ahau Kin.

Mayan myth tells how the hero twins Hunahpu and Xbalanque played the ball game so often that they annoyed the gods of Xibalba, the underworld. These gods of death challenged the boys to a round of the game down in their world. The boys accepted and used their cleverness to make their way through the nine layers of Xibalba. They used magic to pass safely through the House of Knives and lit fires to survive the House of Cold. The twins went on to win the ballgame. But their real victory came when they tricked the gods by demonstrating their ability to cut themselves into pieces and reassemble their own bodies. The gods begged the twins to perform this amazing feat on them, too. The twins gladly did as they asked—sort of. After sufficiently chopping up the gods, the twins left them that way. Having outwitted the death gods, the twins were reborn as the sun and moon.

With whom did the Maya share their myths and deities?

After the Mayan civilization declined, some of its beliefs and culture (as well as those of the ancient Olmecs, who had lived in present-day Mexico and Guatemala from about 1200 B.C.E.) were adopted by later Mesoamerican peoples. A people called the Toltecs flourished from about 900 to 1150. Then, around 1325, a civilization known as the Aztecs began building the city of Tenochtitlan. This great city, built on an island in a lake, became the center of an empire that covered a vast area of Mesoamerica.

The Aztecs had a very religious society, whose beliefs both inspired their greatness and led to their downfall. Motivated by their desire for items such as seashells and obsidian (a sharp volcanic glass used to make knife blades), which were used in religious ceremonies, the Aztecs built a trading network that extended throughout Mexico. The Aztecs also waged constant wars against neighboring cities in order to expand their empire and capture victims for their religious sacrifices. Aztec rule over conquered peoples was harsh—for those who survived—and their list of enemies grew long. When Spanish invaders arrived in 1519, they found many Aztec neighbors willing to help overthrow the empire.

From what were the earth and sky created?

The Aztecs believed that four world eras, called suns, existed before their own. Confrontations between the gods, especially Quetzalcoatl, the benevolent god of the winds, learning, and the planet Venus, and Tezcatlipoca, the mysterious god of night and sorcery, led to the destruction and creation of these suns. Quetzalcoatl and Tezcatlipoca were constantly at odds over who would rule the universe. The two opposing gods represented good and evil, light and dark, production and destruction.

In the fifth sun, Quetzalcoatl and Tezcatlipoca looked down from heaven into the watery world. They were horrified to see a ferocious beast with many toothy, hungry mouths and snapping

jaws. This was the monster goddess Tlaltecuhtli. Quetzalcoatl
and Tezcatlipoca decided they would have to get rid of the beast
before creating any beings for the fifth sun, or Tlaltecuhtli
would only devour them all. The two gods transformed
themselves into giant serpents and descended to the vast ocean
where Tlaltecuhtli swam. Quetzalcoatl and Tezcatlipoca each
grabbed hold of one of the monster's feet and gave a mighty
yank in either direction, splitting the goddess in two. The two
creator gods then used one half of Tlaltecuhtli's body to create
the earth and the other half to fashion the sky.

The other gods felt sorry for Tlaltecuhtli and tried to make up
for the way she'd been treated. They created plants, trees,
flowers, caves, rivers, and mountains from her body. The gods
determined that Tlaltecuhtli would provide the things humans
needed for life. In return for these gifts, the gods were said to
demand human flesh and blood. The Aztecs obliged, so human
sacrifice became a significant part of their religion and ritual.
Only human flesh and blood, the Aztecs believed, could
appease Tlaltecuhtli and keep her producing the fruits and
grains needed for human survival. The Aztecs also believed that
human blood contained a precious liquid called *chalchihuatl*,
the only suitable nourishment for the gods.

Many Mesoamerican peoples worshipped the mythological figure Quetzalcoatl in various forms and functions, before he was adopted by the Aztecs. The Aztecs themselves had many descriptions of Quetzalcoatl. At different times, he was worshipped as the wind god, as the kind god of learning and crafts, and as the god of twins. He was the god of Venus, the morning and evening star, but also a god hero who gave his people maize (corn) and the calendar. To make things even more confusing, the mythical Quetzalcoatl is difficult to separate from a real Toltec priest-king who ruled under the same name in the tenth century.

Why are some humans tall and others short?

To populate the fifth sun, the gods sent Quetzalcoatl to Mictlan, the underworld, to collect the bones of a man and a woman from the earlier suns. Mictlantecuhtli, the lord of the underworld, promised Quetzalcoatl the bones, but only if he could play a solid horn. Quetzalcoatl outwitted him by asking worms to hollow out the horn and getting bees to roar and buzz inside it. Having completed the lord's task, the bones were his. Quetzalcoatl took them and ran, but he promptly stumbled into a pit the lord's servants had dug to thwart his escape. Quetzalcoatl's fall caused the bones to scatter. Some broke, and others were nibbled by the birds of the underworld. Quetzalcoatl managed to

Once humans were created, the gods asked one another what the humans would eat. Quetzalcoatl changed himself into an ant and brought kernels of corn from Food Mountain. The gods sampled the corn and decided it was an agreeable source of strength and nourishment. Lightning then split open Food Mountain, releasing corn, beans, and the seeds of other foods for humans to cultivate and eat.

gather the pieces of bone and carry them to the sky, where the goddess Cihuacoatl ground them into a powder and mixed it with blood of the other gods to create the first humans. Because the bones from Mictlan had been broken, humans are different sizes. And because the bones were partly eaten, humans are mortal.

How did the Aztecs decide where to build their capital city of Tenochtitlan?

The Aztec myth of the founding of Tenochtitlan describes the wanderings of their ancestors after the collapse of Toltec society in the twelfth century. Guided by Huitzilopochtli, the god of war and of the sun, the Aztecs traveled for two hundred years. Just when they were feeling especially down and without faith, Aztec priests received a message from Huitzilopochtli: Build the seat of your empire where you find an eagle perched atop a cactus, eating a snake. In 1325 they found that spot—an island in the center of Lake Texcoco.

Undeterred by the challenging location, the Aztecs built the enormous city of Tenochtitlan ("place of the cactus") on the island. In the sacred center of the city, they constructed great pyramids and temples to honor their gods and perform religious sacrifices. Atop the main pyramid of this Great Temple complex was a shrine dedicated to Huitzilopochtli. The Aztecs built canals and bridges to connect the city to the surrounding land and constructed floating gardens on which to grow crops to feed their growing population. By 1520, Tenochtitlan may have been the largest city in the world, with at least two hundred thousand inhabitants.

Why did Montezuma allow the Spanish to take over Tenochtitlan?

In the perpetual struggle between the gods, Tezcatlipoca managed to drive Quetzalcoatl from Tenochtitlan. Before leaving, Quetzalcoatl ordered his servants to build him a tomb and throw all his treasures into the rivers and canyons.

Quetzalcoatl remained in his tomb for three days, then emerged and left for the land of the dead. On his way there, he fashioned an arrow from one tree and shot it into another tree, forming a cross. Quetzalcoatl said that he would one day return to his people, and this sign would help the people know him. Then he sailed off in a raft made of serpents and became the planet Venus.

The Aztec myth of Quetzalcoatl's return said that the god would eventually come back to them in triumph as a light-skinned, bearded god. Ancestors passed down stories predicting that Quetzalcoatl would come from the east, riding a deer and bearing the cross and jaguar emblems. In 1519 Spanish explorers led by Hernán Cortés arrived in Mesoamerica from the east, on horseback, wearing Christian crosses, and bearing banners adorned with a golden lion of Castile (a region in Spain). The Aztec ruler Montezuma greeted them, thinking Cortés was Quetzalcoatl returning. Instead, the Spaniards were invaders in search of gold and riches. Montezuma let himself be captured, and by 1521 the Spanish had conquered the entire Aztec empire.

Pyramid of Quetzalcoatl in Teotihuacán, Mexico

SOUTH AMERICA

Where did the most sophisticated cultures of South America live?

South America's largest and most highly organized societies grew up in the Andes Mountains, along the western edge of the continent. Several civilizations flourished in this area in the centuries before Europeans arrived. We know little of these cultures' mythologies because South American peoples did not develop a writing system and because many myths were adopted and adapted by the Inca, the dominant civilization in South America for a century before the Spanish arrived in 1532.

Who were the Incas' most important gods?

Chief among their gods was Viracocha, an all-powerful creator god who had been worshipped, in various forms, by many earlier South American cultures. Viracocha was said to be ever present, mysterious, and invisible, but he was sometimes represented as an old, bearded man wearing a long robe.

According to one myth, Viracocha created a world of darkness, into which he brought humans, animals, plants, and other gods. He fashioned the humans from clay and distinguished each nation by painting different clothes on them and giving them distinctive customs, languages, songs, and seeds for planting. Viracocha breathed life into his creations and told them to descend into the earth and appear on its surface through caves, lakes, and hills. This the people did, and built temples at these places where they had entered the world. Then Viracocha ordered the sun, moon, and stars to rise into the sky and bring light into the world. He bestowed upon the first Inca ruler, Manco Capac, a headdress and battle-ax as the symbols of royalty.

After creating the world, Viracocha traveled his lands as a hero figure, shaping the landscape and teaching people the arts of civilization. After this Viracocha became more distant, leaving the rule of everyday life to other gods. The most important of these deities were Mama Kilya, the moon goddess; Ilyap'a, the god of thunder and weather; and Inti, the sun god.

To whom was the Inca emperor related?

The Inca royal family was said to be descended from Inti, the deity at the center of Inca religion and mythology. According to some myths, Inti's son Manco Capac became the first Inca ruler. He married his sister Mama Coya, who became the first Inca queen. Manco Capac and all kings after him were regarded as the "son of the sun."

The strong association between the sun god and the Inca king, known as the Sapa Inca, strengthened the king's claim to rule and helped him hold the Inca Empire together. Conquered peoples were allowed to retain their own beliefs and religions, as long as they accepted the Sapa Inca's divine status. The Inca often adapted myths of their conquered neighbors and altered them to fit in with the Inca worldview.

What did the Inca see flying in the friendly skies?

In the high peaks of the Andes, where mountaintops seemed to almost touch the heavens, sky gods were especially important. Inca mythology makes many links between earthly creatures and events and their counterparts in the skies. For example, an eclipse of the moon was believed to occur because a great serpent or mountain lion was attempting to eat the likeness of Mama Kilya. To scare off the hungry creature, the Inca made as much noise as possible.

The Milky Way, which appears in the night sky as a hazy band of milky white stars, was thought to be a river from which Ilyap'a drew water. This water was stored in a jug and only fell to the earth as rain when Ilyap'a shattered the jug with a lightning bolt loosed from his slingshot. Thunder was said to be the snap of his weapon; lightning was the flash his clothes made as he moved.

Stars and constellations were also important, as they were considered lesser gods and protectors of various earthly activities. One Inca myth said that when the constellation Yacana (the Llama) disappeared from the sky at midnight, it was drinking water from the earth and thus preventing floods. Other animal constellations—there was thought to be one depicting each kind of animal and bird on earth—were responsible for nurturing their earthly equivalents.

On the snowcapped Andean peaks, human sacrifices were made to Viracocha and other major gods. These sacrifices were offered on the most special occasions, such as the coronation of a new king. The sacrificed person, often a child, became a direct representative of the people and lived forever with the gods. Often the bodies of these sacrificed people were mummified by the cold, dry mountain air. In 1999 scientists discovered the well-preserved mummies of three children, two girls and a boy, high in the Andes.

Was there an El Dorado?

Gold and silver had deep religious meaning to the Incas, who considered these precious metals to be the sweat of the sun and the tears of the moon. Many objects, including the doors and walls of the Temple of the Sun in Cuzco, were *gilded*, or covered with a thin layer of gold. Craftsmen also made fine gold jewelry and figurines.

Stories of gold and silver treasures fueled the imagination and greed of Spanish explorers who arrived in South America in the sixteenth century. The most captivating tale of all was the myth of El Dorado, the Golden Man, who was said to be ruler of a

kingdom of gold, a kingdom whose wealth was far greater than any in the world.

The story of such a kingdom was grounded in fact, as it was the custom of one South American tribe to honor each new chief by covering him with gold dust. The chief washed off the gold in a sacred lake while he and his people threw in more gold. The custom ended long before the Spanish arrived, and no kingdom of El Dorado was ever found.

But the fantastic story lives on.

Ramachandra on the sea

Calling out over thousands of years, myths from civilizations long gone still have the power to mystify and amaze us. But there was a time when these stories were nearly lost—or at least hidden out of sight.

For more than a thousand years, people had stopped telling the myths. During medieval times, as Christianity grew more powerful in Europe, the old ideas about myths were thought to be evil. The Christian church tried to stamp out all worship of the old gods and goddesses. In places like Greece and Egypt, old temples to gods and goddesses were destroyed and burned to erase any sign of the old myths.

Then there was a great change during the time we call the Renaissance—a word that means "rebirth." Starting in the 1300s, many of the old ideas of Greece and Rome, lost for a thousand years, were rediscovered in old books and writings. Poets and writers began to learn about the old stories once more. Artists who had only painted pictures of religious scenes soon began to depict characters from mythology, such as Botticelli's *Birth of Venus*.

As time went by, a new science called *archaeology* began to uncover ancient places, like the location of Troy, and unlock the secrets hidden inside the Pyramids. As people learned more about the world of the past, the old tales of mythology—once nearly forgotten—were reborn into our culture.

Today we can see the legacy of myths all around us. Our calendars, the names of the stars and planets, and our everyday language are filled with words that came from myths. But the best part about myths is that we love to keep telling them. Whether it is the story of a boy who wants to fly and do magic—like Harry Potter or Luke Skywalker—or a human with animal powers—like Spiderman—people still tell new and different versions of these ancient tales. J. R. R. Tolkien, the author of *The Lord of the Rings*, spent his life studying myths and legends. His story of a Hobbit who goes on a great quest owes much to the ancient legends.

Myths can show us that gods and heroes can be foolish and make the same mistakes that humans make. But others teach us important lessons about bravery, loyalty, courage, and honor. People have always needed heroes. The great myths also teach us that, like our heroes, it *is* okay to have great dreams and grand hopes.

Myths are also one of the best ways to see that we humans are more alike than different. And that is a very important lesson in a world that is often torn apart by differences of religion, race, and culture. Underneath it all, myths are about that innate human curiosity that we all share—curiosity about people, the world, the heavens.

I hope that this book—like the books I read when I was back in fifth grade—has sparked the same sense of curiosity and amazement about the world of myths. After all, it is the questions we ask about the world around us that have taken humanity from the dark caves of prehistoric times to the outermost edges of the universe.

And that's no myth!

Bierhorst, John. *The Mythology of Mexico and Central America*. New York: William Morrow, 1990.

Bierlein, J. F. *Living Myths*. New York: Ballantine Wellspring, 1999.

———. *Parallel Myths*. New York: Ballantine Wellspring, 1994.

Bulfinch, Thomas. *Bulfinch's Mythology*. New York: Random House, 1993.

Campbell, Joseph. *The Hero with a Thousand Faces*. Princeton, NJ: Princeton University Press, 1972.

———. *The Power of Myth*. New York: Anchor Books, 1990.

———. *Transformations of Myth Through Time*. New York: HarperCollins, 1990.

Cotterell, Arthur, and Rachel Storm. *The Ultimate Encyclopedia of Mythology*. London: Lorenz Books, 1999.

D'Aulaire, Ingri, and Edgar D'Aulaire. *Book of Greek Myths*. New York: Dell, 1962.

Dryden, John, trans. *Virgil's Aeneid*. New York: P. F. Collier, 1937.

Fagles, Robert, trans. *The Iliad*. New York: Viking, 1990.

———, trans. *The Odyssey*. New York: Viking, 1996.

Hamilton, Edith. *Mythology*. New York: Penguin Books, 1942.

Husain, Shahrukh. *Demons, Gods & Holy Men from Indian Myths & Legends*. New York: Peter Bedrick Books, 1987.

January, Brendan. *The New York Public Library Amazing Mythology*. New York: John Wiley, 2000.

Jay, Roni. *Teach Yourself Mythology*. Chicago: NTC Publishing Group, 1996.

The Kingfisher Book of Mythology. New York: Kingfisher, 2001.

Leeming, David Adams. *The World of Myth*. New York: Oxford University Press, 1990.

McIntosh, Jane, and Clint Twist. *Civilizations: Ten Thousand Years of Ancient History*. New York: DK, 2001.

Narayan, R. K. *The Mahabharata: A Shortened Modern Prose Version of the Great Indian Epic*. New York: Viking, 1978.

Osborne, Mary Pope. *Favorite Norse Myths*. New York: Scholastic, 1996.

Parrinder, Geoffrey. *African Mythology*. New York: Peter Bedrick Books, 1967.

Philip, Neil. *The Illustrated Book of Myths*. New York: DK, 1995.

———. *Mythology*. New York: Alfred A. Knopf, 1999.

Philippi, Donald L., trans. *Kojiki*. Princeton, NJ, and Tokyo: Princeton University Press and University of Tokyo Press, 1969.

Sandars, N. K., trans. *The Epic of Gilgamesh*. New York: Penguin Books, 1972.

Tedlock, Dennis, trans. *Popol Vuh: The Definitive Edition of the Mayan Book of the Dawn of Life and the Glories of Gods and Kings*. New York: Simon & Schuster, 1985.

Terry, Patricia, trans. *Poems of the Vikings: The Elder Edda*. Indianapolis, IN: Bobbs-Merrill, 1969.

Willis, Roy, ed. *World Mythology*. London: Duncan Baird, 1993.

Wood, Marion. *Myths and Civilization of the Native Americans*. New York: Peter Bedrick Books, 1998.

References to photos and illustrations are in *italics*.